You Raise Me Up

Making It Happen for Children of the Ark

Catherine Ritch

Photography by
Mark L. Barden

CRM BOOKS
Publishing Hope for Today's Society
Inspirational Books~CDs~Children's Books

CRM BOOKS; PO Box 935, Indian Trail, NC 28079

Visit our Web site at www.ciridmus.com

Printed in the United States of America

ISBN (10 digit): 1-933341-39-4

ISBN (13 digit): 9781933341392

LCCN: 2014936021

To the beautiful people of
Armenia and
Nagorno-Karabakh,
Project AGAPE
And all those
who have been,
are,
and continue to be
responsible for its ability
to serve thousands of people
in a disputed territory
forgotten by the
rest of the world

A Special Thanks

A special thanks goes to Nara Melkonyan, whose selfless dedication and work with Project AGAPE over the past 17 years has literally made a change for the better in the world of thousands of residents of the Kashatagh province and its border villages in the Republic of Nagorno-Karabakh, a disputed territory not even recognized by the United Nations and that, due to political situations, is ignored by the rest of the world.

Nara's dream was to be an Ambassador, but she gave up her own desires to follow the path she felt God called her to undertake. In walking that path, she has truly become one of the world's great ambassadors.

Nara, may you continue to see "God's hand at work" and may you also continue to be "God's hand at work!"

ACKNOWLEDGMENTS

To the entire Project AGAPE staff for your continual help and support while I was in Armenia. You are a wonderfully blessed team with hearts of love, devotion and service to not only your own country, but to humankind. My deepest thanks to each and every one of you! And especially to those of you who set up my own personal "Garden of Eden" at AGAPE for my writing station. I miss it daily.

To Dr. George Aynilian for introducing me and opening my eyes to an unknown history of Armenia when this book was first an idea, and for, like Harry Moorachian and Mary (Maro) Telfeyan, helping to inspire yet another book regarding the history and genocide of Armenia, a story too little known. You share a rich history.

To Rev. Charles and Ann Davis, Suzanne Stafford, Sandy Waldron and Dr. Kyles Wallace for setting the stage with the events that sowed the seeds and cultivated the earliest thoughts for a project of humanitarian aid in Armenia and Nagorno-Karabakh. To me, you shall always be a part of "The Remarkable 9."

To Rev. Alec and Dot Alvord, for your hospitality and invaluable help on the early days of Project AGAPE, and to Darwyn and Jeannine Van Gorp for their help with the transitional days of the project.

To St. John's Lutheran Church, Concord, NC, whose prayers, support and encouragement meant much to the writing of this book, as with everything I do, and for your interest and support in Project AGAPE.

To Bishop Charlene Kammerer, former Bishop of the Western North Carolina Conference of The United Methodist Church for first introducing me to Project AGAPE at Annual Conference years ago; and to Bishop Hope Morgan Ward, North Carolina Conference of The United Methodist Church, who has had a connection with Project AGAPE from its inception. I am most appreciative of your encouragement and helpful advice.

To Steve Taylor, Director of Connectional Ministries for the North Carolina Conference of The United Methodist Church, for all of his experienced information and guidance, and to his secretary, Kathy Duncan, for helping me track down information in the NCC Archives

To Dr. Elizabeth H. Cordes, Rene Henderson, Dr. Steve and Linda Erlandson, Courtney Beals, and Rev. Jamie Armstrong, all of whom have served Project AGAPE in a special way. Thanks for not only sharing your stories and memories with me, but allowing me to use them in this book.

To all the members of work teams who have helped with Project AGAPE since its inception, to all who have contributed monetarily or through donations for distribution, and to the hands who work at the Mission Response Center in Terrell, NC, to make sure items arrive at their destination with no problems in customs clearance

To the mission team of First United Methodist Church, Elkin, NC (WNCC) and the NCC team of 2013 who allowed me to be a part of your experiences while I was in Armenia and Nagorno-Karabakh

To Rev. Allan van Meter, Rev. Cecil Donahue, and past and present members of the Board of Directors of Project AGAPE for your devotion of time and support to carry on this great work, which truly is the epitome of God's "agape" love

To Mark Kushigian for use of his father's story

To Deana Martin and Vera Drye for helping proof the manuscript, and to my mother, Corene Ritch, for the many hours of reading behind me as I typed to meet the deadlines. This could not have happened without your comments, prayers and support.

And to Nara Melkonyan for our round-the-clock conversations (via email and Skype) over the past several weeks to be sure I had correct spellings, translations and information, all while carrying on your hectic work of distributions and usual responsibilities at Project AGAPE. This book would have never happened if not for your dear friendship and support. You are one of the most amazing people I know!

Lastly, to Rev. Mark Barden for introducing me to Nara Melkonyan years ago, and for planting a seed of desire to make the story of Project AGAPE known to the world, most of whom have never even heard of Armenia, much less Nagorno-Karabakh. For your professional photography, as always, and for your sense of mission and honest feedback, I am eternally grateful. Your pictures add a whole different dimension to these pages.

A Note from the Author

I typically do not write the note to my readers until a book is completed and ready for press. However, as I sit just outside Yerevan watching the sun go down behind Mount Ararat from the advantageous viewpoint of the Arch of Charents (which offers the most breathtaking view of the Ararat Valley and Mount Ararat of anywhere), I feel compelled to share with you how I came upon this particular title for the book.

Last night, I was an invited guest— along with the work team from First United Methodist Church, Elkin, North Carolina and Nara's entire immediate family—at the home of Nara's mother. After a delicious and relaxing Sunday evening meal, and while the hostesses began clearing the table for dessert, I was asked to play the piano. After a few selections, I asked Nara—also an accomplished pianist—to join me. And then, grateful for the opportunity to hear someone else play for a change, I left her to play for our enjoyment. She first played a few pieces from her native culture, all of which were absolutely beautiful yet unrecognizable to our party of Americans. Then she began to play a simple but stirring melody, which I immediately recognized as *You Raise Me Up*. I began to sing the text in my head and then moved back to the piano to join her in a duet of the piece the entire group now recognized. As we approached the last phrase, I looked up at everyone and exclaimed, "That's it! That's the title!" They all instantly agreed that it was a perfect title, and it worked with the subtitle for which I had been accumulating facts for the book during the past several months.

I still wanted to sleep on the idea that evening and until the group left to return to America the next morning, and I had time to stay in Armenia and think quietly and uninterruptedly. The more I contemplated, the more suited that title seemed for the story. Nara later said the same thing. That was the deciding vote. I was now assured that there was a book well underway in my laptop now titled *You Raise Me Up: Making It Happen for Children of the Ark.* The four words "You raise me up" were a perfect match between the story I was attempting to portray and the imagery of raising one up— whether that story be the ark on the flood waters, or the mission of Project AGAPE working with the people of the Nagorno-Karabakh region.

In my interview with Rev. Charles Davis regarding his initial three-month visit to Armenia, leading to the organization of Project AGAPE, his comment, "What people fail to understand is that when the Soviet Union fell, *everything* fell," was one of the most powerful statements heard during my research. For I have been involved in mission work—locally, nationally and internationally—for decades, but those very words are what set Project AGAPE apart from any other place I have ever been. Besides the fact of its long history of Christianity, its people have endured situations and circumstances unimaginable to most of the world. Because of communism for seven decades, the practice of making decisions for their own well-being and welfare was absent from everyday life of the citizens of Armenia.

Many Americans either have, or have ancestors who have, endured the Great Depression or the Civil War. Stories of "picking themselves up from their bootstraps" are endless and amazing. I, too, have many accounts of those stories in my own family. But it wasn't until the writing of this book—spending five weeks immersed in Armenia and Kashatagh while observing the work of Project AGAPE and learning about the three cataclysmic events that led to its formation—that I began to grasp the fullness of what that "fall" actually entailed, and how it continues to effect the population of Nagorno-Karabakh.

I adored the many ways of connecting with the residents of Nagorno-Karabakh through the work of AGAPE. Music is **always** the same in any language, but making music with the orphans and children at the Children's Home was beyond compare. They loved playing musical games, teaching me Armenian words and writing in my tablets of book notes. We were all one and the same through God's love. No words were necessary, even though my Armenian vocabulary did broaden, thanks to the children.

And then I was allowed to be a part of the "human reindeer" system, taking the reins of the leader behind my neck and around my arms with the three young men who had worked out their own system for unloading the huge shipping container of supplies sent from North Carolina. My neck hurt for months, but it was the best hurt, and although it went away with time, the feeling of God's amazing love from that experience did not. We were connected.

Then to meet Agape—now 18 but who was the first child born in the AGAPE Hospital—when all the children and youth came to receive their "shoeboxes" breathed new life for another generation. And to be able to pass out dolma, its filling the food prepared from packets of the Stop Hunger Now project, for these same children during their "Shoebox" distribution, what an honor! This was no longer work I had read and known about, it was God's love in action, as Project AGAPE was "making it happen" for the residents of Kashatagh.

Through each and every act there, I felt the love that stretched from my home state of North Carolina—and hopefully soon from my home country of America—to our beautiful brothers and sisters in Nagorno-Karabakh, especially in the Kashatagh region of that disputed territory. To anyone who has sent a shoebox, or other donations, or contributed money for a cow or any other program of Project AGAPE, you *are* the face of "agape" love to the people who live there, and your love is reciprocated through the expressions of love and appreciation shown on their faces.

This note began with my earliest writing of this book, and ends with my last two days of writing it. As I penned the ending pages, words and music to a song immediately— as if from nowhere—rushed through my mind. They were words written by David Piner, Executive Director of Arbor Acres, a United Methodist retirement community in Winston-Salem, North Carolina. I was privileged to compose the music for his lyrics to several songs, done as an annual report of the Western North Carolina Annual Conference several years ago. The songs had long been gone from my thoughts, but in typing the last few pages, one of the songs, *We Are Blessed to Be a Blessing*, played over and over in my head as I finished the book. It was not until that moment that I realized the depth of the piece that David and I had jointly written back then. I knew that the moment this book was completed, the song would be pulled from the files of my musical compositions to again find use.

There are so many things learned, and interesting

people, met in the course of each book's research, but this one has provided more than any other of my now twenty-five books in print, and over 60+ more at some point of completion in my computer. I have made numerous new friends, many of them Armenian, and many of those practically in my back door—at least in neighboring states.

One of the most outstanding things I learned, which you will also discover from other's comments as you read this book, is that persons who have worked with Project AGAPE, or been associated with the project, all wish to return. That is no different for me. Fortunately I love to travel, and love sitting in quiet remote places with a view in which to write and meditate. However, if I could hop on a plane at this very moment and go anywhere in the world, it would be to Nagorno-Karabakh where I could again look from my second-floor window, on the very same floor that burned and was reconstructed ten years ago, and listen to the night sounds of the jackals and look over the beautiful mountains of "the land of Ararat."

I pray this title and this book will raise your awareness and call to help others as much as it has mine.

Blessings of peace and God's AGAPE love,

Catherine

Please note that, for the most part,

names of churches and individuals

who have helped with a mission team

are not mentioned in this book.

They are nameless, faceless individuals and entities.

That is purposely so that each church and person

involved in this story may represent you, the reader,

and/or your church or organization.

They are all persons or groups whom God

has blessed with a heart for missions and for others –

a heart accompanied by a helping hand.

Thus, physical attributes are not

the important characteristics here.

May you find yourself,

some way, some day,

inside the pages of this book.

It matters not what country of the world you are in. If you pick up a children's Bible or Bible storybook, you will immediately see a picture of a huge boat with pairs of animals. In all probability, this picture may even be on the book's cover. There will usually be an older-looking bearded man somewhere in the picture, sometimes with a wife, and maybe with three sons and their wives. The scene is oftentimes displayed with a rainbow and a dove holding an olive branch in its mouth. If you are Christian, you will most likely recognize the story simply from the familiar images, even without being able to read the words of any particular language. For those who do not recognize the picture or the story, consider yourself blessed. You have just been introduced to Noah and the Ark . . .

and Armenian history.

PROLOGUE

You Raise Me Up is a story of endurance, survival, tenacity, perseverance and a people choosing death rather than giving up their Christianity. It is a story of the oldest Christian nation in the world, filled with unparalleled history and culture. And it is a story of a disputed territory, the Republic of Nagorno-Karabakh, which was once a part of that nation of Armenia and is now unrecognized even by the United Nations. Whereas other humanitarian agencies have had to withdraw due to political issues with their neighboring countries, two conferences of The United Methodist Church—the North Carolina Conference and the Western North Carolina Conference—have answered a call and have broken those barriers through organizing and

1

supporting Project AGAPE, that area's ONLY humanitarian aid agency, thereby "Making it Happen for Children of the Ark."

We read in the Bible of two times when God called to Noah in this land of Ararat, first in Genesis 6 when God said, "Make yourself an ark," and then explicitly instructed Noah on how to make it. And then again in Genesis 7:1, "Then the Lord said to Noah, 'Go into the ark, you and all your household, for I have seen that you alone are righteous before me in this generation.'"

The scriptures tell us that Noah followed God's call. This book is about another call—different, yet similar—given thousands of years later. Different in that God is calling us to help His hurting children; similar in that His hurting children are in a place that was once a part of that land of Ararat. For you see, the fall of the Soviet Union, and the subsequent war with Azerbaijan over a boundary dispute that still persists as a result of that war, have completely blocked any economic growth or development in this area. Due to that, the average monthly income of the Kashatagh province of Nagorno-Karabakh is the equivalent of $60.00 or less.

The story of Noah ends with "And the ark rested in the seventh month, on the seventeenth day of the month, upon the mountains of Ararat." That verse from Genesis 8:4 (*KJV*) as well as the two preceding chapters, which make mention of certain historical and Biblical figures who choose to flee or escape to "the land of Ararat," serve to demonstrate that we—all humanity—fall into the category of "Children of the Ark." We are a people whose very being and Christianity have developed over the course of history as a result of what took place in this at-one-time prestigious land, the land of Ararat that was then part of Armenia. Though this land covered much of the known world in ancient times, it is now a land little known by others around the world. Yet it is a land that is one of the most controversial spots in the world.

Armenia, also the oldest Christian nation in the world, is therefore a part of our Christian heritage as it is a place where many people answered God's call to them. It is a place historically associated with the rainbow – God's symbol of hope and promise to **all** people. This book is filled with God's call on various individuals who have been instruments in making it happen for the children of the ark. May this book instill in you, the readers, a desire to continue to make it happen for the children of the ark as you learn of the miraculous birth and incredible work of Project AGAPE, a light to the disputed republic of Nagorno-Karabakh, a part of Greater Armenia.

PART ONE

A Miraculous Birth

The Emergence

CHAPTER 1

A City of Light

And it came to pass in those days ... Luke 2:1

Project AGAPE . . . it is frequently referred to as "a city of light" on a hillside. At least that is how it appears to someone approaching Berdzor, the capital of the Kashatagh province of Nagorno-Karabagh, for the first time. Even in the daylight, without the advantage of lighted windows, there is no doubt that from the moment it is first spotted, the vision far off in the distance is calling to be recognized as a beacon of hope for all who enter this land. Oddly, it appears the very same to the nearly 10,000 residents who live in Berdzor or one of the border villages of the area, "for they have seen a great light" on many occasions, through the work and support that comes from the small compound known as Project AGAPE.

There are several aspects about AGAPE that cause it to be a distinctly unique mission project. One, most missions are created to try to win souls to Christ in the process of working with the inhabitants. That is not the case with Project AGAPE. Armenia is the oldest Christian nation in the world, with its first church built in 301 AD; therefore they do not need others to come in and tell them about Christ. What they need are other caring Christians to come and show God's love.

Second, many missions are the direct result of a natural disaster or a single situation. Granted, a natural disaster is a part of AGAPE's inception. For while Americans remember December 7th as Pearl Harbor Day, Armenians remember it as the Wednesday in 1988 when 25,000 men, women and children lost their lives as the result of a catastrophic earthquake. Add to the devastating earthquake another December event, in 1991, when the Soviet Union comes crashing down into 15 separate countries, subsequently leading to a territorial war between the Armenians who had been living in the Kashatagh region of Nagorno-Karabakh and Azerbaijan—which on May 5, 1994 ends in a ceasefire situation. It is the series of these three unfortunate circumstances that catapult the entire region's economic situation into a dire state of poverty. And not only that, this resulting state of affairs completely blocks the economic growth and development of the area.

Third, because of the political ramifications surrounding Nagorno-Karabakh, Project AGAPE— a religious humanitarian organization, which has been invited by the Armenian Apostolic Church and registered by the State

Council of RA (Republic of Armenia) Committee on Religious Affairs—is the **only** agency that does humanitarian aid work in this disputed territory. From the beginning of Nagorno-Karabakh's independence, other well-known agencies have to withdraw their humanitarian aid support for if they had stayed, they would have lost their right to work in certain other countries where they had a larger base. Therefore, for this troubled area, theirs is a story for which only God could be the Author as numerous and miraculous doors continue to open for the work of the American, Greater Armenian Partnership Effort. (It should be noted that AGAPE was originally founded as the American Georgian Armenian Partnership Effort, but because the needs of this disputed territory were so great, it was decided that all efforts should be focused totally on Kashatagh as financial means would not allow both areas to be adequately served.)

In addition, there are currently thousands of Syrian refugees fleeing to Armenia, many within the borders of Nagorno-Karabakh (historically called "Artsakh"). Because of the countless number of Armenians who fled to Syria during the Armenian genocide of 1915, they now, in return, accept those who once protected their ancestors. This creates a growing population in this area that, two years ago, was only pushing 8,000 residents.

The Armenians now control the disputed territory, however, and the Nagorno-Karabakh flag is exactly the same as the Armenian flag except for a wide white zigzagged band running through the red, blue and orange stripes to signify that the two territories have been torn apart. In

Stepanakert, the capital of Nagorno-Karabakh, stands a large statue of Grandmother and Grandfather Armenia. Only the faces of an elderly man and woman, both draped in historic Armenian headdress and carved from red rock, stick up out of the ground. This sculpture symbolizes that the rest of their bodies are grounded in historic and ancient Armenian soil.

So as not to get bogged down, it is easier to understand and accept that here are God's children, children of the ark, who are our Christian brothers and sisters and who are in unspeakably desperate need and poverty. Noah was given a call to build an ark and take his family inside to survive the flood; we are given a call to reach out to the people of that ancient land of Ararat who have now survived a flood of cataclysmic ordeals and help them rebuild their lives and homes that still sit in the shadow of Mount Ararat. Our call is to show God's unconditional love to our hurting and needy brothers and sisters, explained as "agape" love in the New Testament.

The dictionary offers two definitions for the word "agape." One, derived from the New Testament, is selfless unconditional love, expecting nothing in return, as Christ loves us. There happens to be another definition of the word "agape," this pronunciation with two syllables instead of three. That is when the mouth is open due to wonder or amazement. There is no doubt that kind of wonder and amazement is present on the faces of anyone who has ever heard the stories, both chilling and heartwarming, of the work done by Project AGAPE, not to mention the amount of love that flows from that work. Thus, aptly named,

Project AGAPE depicts a beautiful illustration of both of those definitions. It is a perfect example of the definition of God's agape love for humankind, and humankind's love for God in return. One of the expressions of that agape love is demonstrated to our brothers and sisters in Armenia through sending useful and necessary items to the people of Nagorno-Karabakh, as well as work teams to work hand-in-hand with them to build a better environment. And it is the expression of God's love, through a partnership between the North Carolina Conference and the Western North Carolina Conference of The United Methodist Church, in conjunction with the Armenian Apostolic Church that gives birth to Project AGAPE and keeps it going. Skeptics gave it five years; it has now been thriving and growing for 20 years and it is still going strong, thanks to the relentless efforts of those who first visited Armenia and Nagorno-Karabakh to access the needs and discover how to best help the people.

Although launched in 1993, it is actually 1994 when Project AGAPE officially receives its first state registration. Therefore, it is celebrating its 20th anniversary this year. This is also a special milestone for it comes one year before the 100th anniversary of the Armenian genocide. Now, after two decades, the project continues to serve hundreds of the area's families, thousands of people, through various projects and areas of ministry.

Building teams continue to help with improvements to local housing, in everything from reconstructing burned-out shells, to putting on tin roofs, or sometimes replacing tarp as the only protection from elements of nature. They also continue to work with the Children's Home, the Christian Education Center, and the AGAPE Hospital and clinics on any necessary additions, and by providing improvements with sanitation for the area.

Warehouse distribution plays an important role in the mission of Project AGAPE. From its first days, a warehouse is acquired in Yerevan, with the main focus being on the distribution of blankets and coats. The project has greatly expanded and although there is still an office in Yerevan, the warehouse is now on the premises of Project AGAPE's Berdzor site and includes the distribution of clothes, shoes, furniture, blankets, fabrics and supplies for sewing, toiletries and many other items needed by the local residents of both the town and the outlying villages. As well as assisting the local families of these areas, the warehouse donations also help the AGAPE Christian Education Center, the Children's Home and Orphanage, the hospital and clinics, the veterinary station and it provides school supplies to the two local schools.

Monetary contributions help pay the salaries of the local priest of the Armenian Apostolic Church, the veterinarian who works with AGAPE's Cattle Project, the head doctor of the AGAPE hospital, teachers for the Christian Education Center, and the AGAPE staff, as well as paying for the operational costs of office space, transportation expenses and upkeep of vehicles.

The local government of the area is most supportive of Project AGAPE. By working closely with the area administration, and also with the Armenian Apostolic Church, the project is able to help far more people than if working alone. The project collects Christmas Shoeboxes for the children, who would otherwise receive nothing at Christmas, and distributes them each year near January 6th (the day Armenians observe Christmas), along with sponsoring a wonderful celebration for the birth of Christ. The Cattle Project helps families to provide for themselves with dairy products and by breeding the heifers to help pass on calves to other families. Although Heifer International is unable to help Nagorno-Karabakh, their principles of making the animal husbandry process work have been adopted by the Cattle Project, thereby making sure that recipients of the cows get the proper training for raising and breeding the cows, as well as the veterinary services that are necessary for the project's success.

Christian education is a key element, and one of the most used resources, in the work of Project AGAPE. Therefore, the Christian Education Center is understandably home to many areas of training that are not a part of the regular school curriculum. One time, only because of a lack of funds during 2013, the center closes for several months. However, thanks to the support of the North Carolina Conference, all of the positions for teachers and instructors are once again filled and the after-school education and programs are again fully operational. One of the amazing factors about AGAPE is that people believe in its work so much that the teachers, the priest, the veterinarian—all of the principal leaders in making the project work—have done their jobs without pay when there has been a lack of funds. Their hearts are totally and unmistakably grounded in the mission of providing Christian leadership and training for the residents of the area, particularly the children and youth.

Some of the courses offered through the Christian Education Center are computer classes, which have provided appropriate instruction to allow some of the area adults to find jobs with the government's administrative offices located in Berdzor. Another helpful enterprise for the women has been the sewing classes that have enabled them to make a business of making shirts, pants and other items for the locals. Traditional cultural arts, such as cross-stitch and rug-making, are also taught. For mental challenges, chess is also part of the curriculum. (An interesting tidbit about the country of Armenia is that it is not uncommon to see men, sitting at small tables lining the streets or stuck in an unobtrusive alleyway, totally absorbed in a chess game. This helps explain why many of the world chess champions are Armenian.) Music is another area of interest for the Christian Education Center. For children and youth who need help with their studies, tutoring is offered.

The AGAPE Hospital and clinics are a most instrumental aspect of the project. The leadership and spiritual guidance, as well as the medical knowledge and experience, of "Dr. Artsakh," Head Doctor of the AGAPE Hospital, has much to do with that. (Born Dalton Buniatyan, the former fighter pilot and military surgeon is so impassioned by his native homeland that he legally changes his given name—even on his passport—to "Artsakh" following the war with Azerbaijan. His children even change his name on their own legal documents) He and his fine staff have made a huge difference for the area of Nagorno-Karabakh. There has been a very supportive relationship between the Armenian Apostolic Church and the United Methodist Church from the onset of Project AGAPE. There at their invitation, we have worked closely in partnership with them in all of the work that has taken place in Armenia.

There is one facet about Nagorno-Karabakh with which there is absolutely no dispute. It matters not whom you speak with, whether uttered in humbled awe by a visiting team member at their first encounter of the project's work, or joyfully proclaimed by a staff member or recipient who has witnessed the project's work countless times, the resounding comment regarding Project AGAPE is always the same: "God's hand at work!" And invariably, the work of God's hand comes in the form of love ... agape love to be precise.

It is no wonder the first baby born in the area's hospital was named Agape. Now 18 years old and a beautiful young lady, she personifies the miraculous wonder of the work begun here 20 years ago, a little longer unofficially. Likewise, a resident of Berdzor offers a litany at one of the Christmas Celebrations. A father of nine children, he and his family live in a bombed-out shelter until after the birth of his eighth child. Thanks to Project AGAPE, he and his family now live in a government-assisted housing project. His exact words are, "It's no accident the name of the project is AGAPE. The name says it all."

Perhaps the best way to understand Project AGAPE, the work it does and the people it serves is to allow the reader an inside look at it through the eyes of its workers and recipients. There is a hymn, *We've a Story to Tell to the Nations.* A portion of its text is as follows:

We've a story to tell to the nations,
That shall turn their hearts to the right,
A story of truth and mercy,
A story of peace and light,
A story of peace and light.
For the darkness shall turn to dawning,
And the dawning to noonday bright;
And Christ's great kingdom shall come on earth,
The kingdom of love and light.

We've a song to be sung to the nations,
That shall lift their hearts to the Lord,
A song that shall conquer evil
And shatter the spear and sword,
And shatter the spear and sword.
For the darkness shall turn to dawning,
And the dawning to noonday bright;
And Christ's great kingdom shall come on earth,
The kingdom of love and light.

The people of Nagorno-Karabakh also have a story, but theirs should be aptly titled, *We've a Story to Tell from the Nation.* It, like the original hymn's text, is a story of truth and mercy, peace and light. It is a song that has conquered evil and shattered the spear and sword, or in their case, guns and tanks. For yes, in their disputed territory, the darkness has turned to dawning, and the dawning is turning to noonday bright, for Christ's great kingdom has come on earth through the love and light of Project AGAPE.

As the baby Agape has grown in strength and stability, so has the project for which she was named. Listen to the story of this great ministry from the voices of those who are a part of it, from its humblest beginnings to those who carry on its mission today, 20 years later. Hear their message as Project AGAPE continues to encourage and empower the now nearly 10,000 residents who still look upon this beacon of hope, a city of light on a hillside.

CHAPTER 2

The Chess Board

And there were in the same country ... Luke 2:8

Imagine yourself in a room with three total strangers and an empty chess board. Although the three of them know each other well, and have already played the game together, you are here in their midst solely because of one thing. You all have a common interest . . . Armenia . . . one of the strongest chess nations in the world, with the most chess grandmasters per capita of any country.

You—like the other three—are not here today to play chess, although you all do have something in common with Tigran Petrosian, the 1963 World Chess Champion from Armenia, whose triumph not only popularized the game of chess in his country, but "led to an outpouring of patriotic fervor" in the Soviet's smallest republic. You all possess an outpouring of fervor for this same smallest republic that was once one of the three largest countries in the world. However your fervor is not patriotic; it is humanitarian.

Although Petrosian was nicknamed "Tigran the Great" after Tigranes the Great (the emperor under whom Armenia, for a short while, became the strongest state east of the Roman Republic), there is no king in this game. The queen, which—if asked by the residents of the Kashatagh region of Nagorno-Karabakh—could be represented by Nara Melkonyan (the Armenian Country Director for Project AGAPE). But she is absent from this meeting so that game piece is also missing. The rook, formerly called the castle, is no more for it comes crashing down with the fall of the Soviet Union. The fall of the rook, however, allows the bishop to move into action on the board, for once the Soviet falls, communism no longer bans the practice of Christianity in Armenia. The knight could be considered one of the strangers in the room due to his three years of travel in all directions over the country of Armenia and the disputed Nagorno-Karabakh. But this stranger, Rev. Charles Davis, realizes God was in charge of his moves and he was "only trying to keep up."

So, in fact, there IS a king, or in this instance, the Grandmaster. This King is God and all the strangers in the room—you included—are merely His pawns on a chess board, which is no longer empty. The chess board has a name . . . Project AGAPE.

When you ask how the chess game, in this case Project AGAPE, gets its start, the response is a cacophony of group laughter from the three strangers. From that moment on, there is an even playing field, or board, for in that laughter is an unspoken and mutual understanding that none of them had anything to do with the start of this game, not to mention the sequence of moves soon to follow. They are simply the playing pieces, the pawns that God moves to where necessary to act as His hands with a servant's heart.

It is quickly apparent that although the chess board is named Project AGAPE, this particular match is called "God's Hands." For when you ask anyone about the project, no matter where and no matter at what point in time of the project's existence, you get the same answer: "God's Hands" or "God's Hand at work." There is no doubt of the identity of the "Grandmaster" here.

Once the laughter from moments before dies down, and the proverbial "ice" is not only broken but melted—through the bond of a common love for God and God's people—the strangers each take their position on the board.

The first stranger, Dr. Suzanne Stafford, shares her role and how she comes to be one of the pawns. She is finishing her PhD in International Development, with a focus on the US and the Soviet Union, at the University of California in Berkeley in the late 1970s when she sends her mother a copy of her resume. It is her very first resume for a job and she sends it for the sole purpose of saying, "Look what I've done, Mom. You'll be proud of me!"

Suzanne's mother, being the poster child for The United Methodist Church who eats, sleeps and breathes

Methodism, promptly sends the resume to The General Board of Global Ministries on Riverside Drive in New York City. With it is a note that reads, "This is my daughter's education. I think she'd make a great missionary. Call her."

Subsequently, Suzanne receives a phone call from Steve Brimigion who says, "Ms. Stafford, I'm the Chief Financial Officer for The General Board of Global Ministries of The United Methodist Church. I want to come interview you."

"How did you get my number?" she asks in shock.

"Your mother gave it to me when she sent us your resume," he replies. Up until that point, Suzanne has no idea her mother has sent out her resume so she is still reeling when the man asks, "I'd like to speak with you. I'm going to be in San Francisco next Tuesday. Would you have lunch with me?"

Suzanne graciously accepts the invitation, thinking she will later take this up with "Mama." During lunch the next Tuesday, Steve Brimigion asks, "Are you interested in a job?"

"No," Suzanne manages to answer politely. "I've just accepted a job with Bank of America Corporate Headquarters." Considering it is the first time the bank has an East European/Soviet division, and that the job provides her a way for promoting US-Soviet friendship and economic cooperation, she is naturally excited about her new position for which she is now well prepared.

Steve, though, continues to stay in touch with her, calling every few months and always asking, "What are you doing now? Are you still happy with your job?"

Her reply is always the same . . . a polite, "Yes."

The lighthearted laughter of the group of strangers, which has been going on through all of this relaying of information stops as Suzanne's playful mood suddenly takes on a serious air, hinting at a change in direction on the chess board. "But it's God's hand here," Suzanne goes on to explain, using the term that has come to be the unified and unrehearsed slogan of Project AGAPE. "A divorce happened, so I either had to have my mother come to the west coast and keep my children or I had to pack up and move back to North Carolina. I knew there was no way my mother could handle San Francisco so I gave up my wonderful job and decided that once I was settled on the east coast, I'd start my own business working with US companies who were setting up businesses in the Soviet Union. A couple of attorneys were the only ones providing that service at that point in time so there was a market for my expertise.

"One day shortly after my move, I got a call from this same Steve Brimigion informing me that a woman, a United Methodist woman, in Texas had died and left the General Board a million dollars to set up a United Methodist Humanitarian Relief for the Soviet Union." Suzanne pauses as she makes eye contact with each of the others in the room. "This is early 1988. A million dollars could do a lot of good for those people." She then goes on with the story. "Mr. Brimigion concluded by asking, 'Ms. Stafford, would you like to fly to New York and talk to Dr. Nugent, General Secretary of the General Board of Global Ministries and myself?'"

Her thoughts, before she answers, still focus on the

fact that a lot of good could be done with that much money; yet it is a big country and they need help any way you touch it. She has already been to visit the area and is aware of the plight of the republics, about poor Armenia that is already beyond destitute, so she listens to her heart—and the "Grandmaster." She goes to New York, where she accepts the humanitarian consultancy position with GBGM, answering directly to Dr. Nugent.

"This is what is really important," she stops to stress to the other pawns, "my job included nothing pastoral or religious; its mandate is totally humanitarian. You need to understand that about my role. So," she continues, "in setting up this relationship, after doing lots of research over there, I recommended The United Methodist Church have two introductory and cooperating partners, the Russian Orthodox Church and the Soviet Peace Fund, which is a customary practice when entering into any cooperative-helping venture with an emerging economy.

"With the Russian Orthodox Church we worked with Father Ioan, who worked directly with the Patriarch. He was in charge of education and outreach and the whole revision of the Russian Orthodox Church. In that effort, he kept traveling to the United States to see how The United Methodist Church was set up. Following the UMC example, he set up the Russian Orthodox kindergartens based on our UMC preschool and kindergarten structure. The Russian Orthodox Women's programs follow our United Methodist Women model, and the list goes on and on.

Armenia enters with meetings set up by Tomas Grigoriev, Director of the Soviet Peace Fund, where

Suzanne is to meet with a representative from each of the 15 republics. At the first meeting, he introduces her and says, "Ms. Stafford, explain how The United Methodist Church wants to work with our republics because we have republics which need a lot of help."

"There was a young lady from Armenia who immediately spoke up, having raised her hand the highest, and said, 'We need help.'

"I asked, 'What kind of help do you need?' and she answered, 'I can't say it. I have to talk to the government. I'll let you know.'

"That was all I heard from Armenia, whereas the representatives from the other countries would state, 'We need da, da, da,' and give a list. But Armenia's representative doesn't say another word. So what do you do, because you can't push?"

The turn of another pawn occurs.

Rev. Charles Davis lives in Moore County, North Carolina, where he pastors the Pleasant Hill United Methodist Church in Robbins. He is nearing retirement and looking forward to enjoying his free time with his lovely wife, Ann. There is the start of a collection of woodworking tools, all of them new and still in the packages, in his garage so his mind—when not on shepherding his congregation—thinks of the many small projects he can begin once he retires. Charles is not your typical minister for he has a military background which includes having been a member of the

Special Forces. After his military days, however, he goes into the ministry and serves churches in the North Carolina Conference of The United Methodist Church. One of Charles' strong points of ministry is his heart for missions and reaching out to others.

Sandy Waldron spends her time serving others, but not necessarily in the ministry or as a humanitarian. She has another role in life. Sandy is a firefighter. Her occupation naturally discloses her concern for others and helping those in need. She is aware that her life could be in danger on any call, as she risks her own to save others. But she clearly understands she is led by "the Grandmaster," so that possibility is never a consideration for her.

As an active member of Pine Grove United Methodist Church in Winston-Salem, North Carolina, she wears many hats in helping with the ministry of her church. But there is one particular job she has. Because she knows how to drive a fire truck, Sandy is often the "designated driver" for the church bus. She is well acquainted with the art of being a pawn, or of being led where God sends her.

Now that there are no longer strangers in your midst in this room, there is one final question regarding this imaginary chess board on which they are positioned and which is seemingly no longer empty. In fact, the board seems to have gotten lots of use since the game began 20 years prior.

"What is your thought on the first move of Project AGAPE?" they are asked.

Suzanne loses no time in answering, "It was the particular time in history and Charles just happened to be that directed, focused person needed for the first move, and his energy, enthusiasm and representation made it all happen." With that one statement, there is no doubt that this threesome is thoroughly engrained, and has been since the first move by "the Grandmaster," in Making it Happen for the Children of the Ark.

CHAPTER 3

They Came from Afar

. . . wise men from the East came, asking . . . Matthew 2:1

It is approximately 1:30 on a Saturday afternoon. Suzanne Stafford stands in her kitchen in Colfax, North Carolina, having just finished lunch. Her thoughts are on the upcoming annual School of Christian Living for the Winston-Salem District of the Western North Carolina Conference, where she will teach a class on *Christianity in the Communist World*. She hopes to make the class interesting and inspiring in order to gain support for the various small Soviet republics, which are struggling horrifically, but most of which are now receiving some service assistance thanks to the million dollar gift left by the woman in Texas.

Now two years after her acceptance of the job as consultant with the General Board of Global Ministries for the Soviet area, the humanitarian efforts, which she oversees, are going full force. Everything is running smoothly. That is, until the phone rings.

"Is this Suzanne Stafford?" she hears from a male voice after picking up the phone and saying, "Hello."

"Yes."

"Ms. Stafford, I'm calling from the Dulles Airport in Washington, DC. Four Armenians are here asking for directions to your home in Colfax. They do not know how to get there. Can you come and pick them up at 3:30?"

Without warning, she laughs. Colfax is 300 miles away from Dulles Airport. She only has two hours to get there. So she answers, "No." But her mind shifts into high gear. "You just tell them to wait right there with you," she quickly informs the man on the phone since the visitors, who must be exhausted after such a long series of flights, are evidently with him at the airport.

This time it is his turn to laugh. "Oh, yes . . . and Ms. Stafford, they do not speak any English. They have a letter they handed to the first person they saw when they got off the plane at the airport. It reads, 'We need to meet with Suzanne Stafford in Colfax, North Carolina. Call her. She will get us.'"

Suzanne gets off the phone and hurls her plan into action. Describing the day, she says, "It so happened The United Methodist Church had organized bringing two very bright students from Russia to Washington, DC, for advanced studies, with one of them securing an internship with the World Bank in Washington, DC. These were two highly educated economists who wanted to help their home country and the former republics climb back on their feet and integrate into the world community of nations.

"I called the two interns and said, 'Guys, payback time! I need you to do me a little favor. I've just rented a van there. I need you to go to Dulles Airport and pick up four gentlemen. They're from Armenia. I have no idea who they are or what they want, but could you pick them up and bring them to my house?'

"So, God bless them," she says, still smiling heartily with the memory, "Vladimir and Sergei went to the airport, picked up the rental van and the four unannounced visitors and drove to Colfax . . . it only took six or seven hours, and the four Armenian gentlemen arrived safely at my house. Each one of them came in lugging two extremely heavy suitcases whose contents clinked. Clinked and sloshed. I had no idea what was inside, but I remember praying that all their belongings were not broken." Suzanne laughs as she continues. "Clinked and sloshed. Two bags each, so that was eight big bags, clinking and sloshing. So, there I was, and so far no idea who they are, or what they're doing here. I'm not about to ask them what's in the bags.

"I simply said, speaking in Russian, 'Gentlemen, you are welcome in my home, we have dinner on the table, and when you have finished, I have your beds set up. Please take a nice long bath and rest. When you get up tomorrow at noon our time, we will talk.

"And sure enough, they ate heartily and said not an exhausted word about why they were here. Their bags were still closed.

"The next day, at lunchtime, we sit down and that's when I finally asked, 'Who are you and why are you here?'

"And they said, 'Ms. Stafford, we're from Armenia. And you said in Mr. Grigoriev's meeting if we need help ...'" Suzanne doesn't even finish repeating their statement. There is no need; the ending is obvious. The awe of the story still overwhelms her, for she knows this is God's hand again.

"And you know what I found?" she asks a few moments later. "I found a letter they had originally sent to me through the Soviet Peace Fund several weeks before their arrival, but had never gotten to me. The letter was in Russian, and asking for critical and emergency help."

She pauses briefly, recalling every detail and making sure not to omit anything. "As it turned out, they were representatives of the Armenian Government and were here to get the United Methodists to help get their people, particularly their women and babies, milk because the country was so destitute. Two of the men were from the Amalgamated Milk Factory, which closed as a result of the fall of the Soviet Union. The other two were bankers, hoping to establish world credit. However, a country has to be in existence for two years before that can happen so I was unable to help them in that capacity. A large number of the neediest of their country were earthquake victims. As a result of the earthquake, they had lost 80% of their dairy herd. Most of the remainder of the cows had been killed for meat, simply to feed their starving population."

Suzanne stops again, shaking her head as she re-lives that conversation with these four Armenians who have shown up without warning. "So I am standing in the kitchen in Colfax with two cats, a dog, two children and these four Armenians, desperately needing help for their country. 'Excuse me, gentlemen,' she says in Russian. 'I've gotta talk to my preacher!

"I called Dr. Kyles Wallace, my minister at Bunker Hill United Methodist Church, and he came right over with Roger Duggins, another member of our congregation. We all sat and talked for a brief while. Kyles and Roger assured them, 'We will be happy to go after milk products for your country. We will help you.'

"That is when the humongous 'clinking' bags came out and were opened. Every bag was full of Armenian Ararat Cognac, Churchill's favorite and regarded as the best cognac in the world. The Ararat Cognac was the most treasured thing they could bring. I was so grateful that Kyles, and a very shocked-looking Roger, managed the understanding and dignity to say, 'Thank you.'

"Shortly after this warm meeting, the guests said, 'Suzanne, you have to take us to the store.' After their initial shocked reaction at encountering a large, well-stocked US supermarket, I suggested that they buy whatever they might need . . . I'll never forget. They bought 23 pounds of meat to make an Armenian Khorovats (barbecue) supper cooked out over an outside fire that night. I invited multiple folk from our congregation, which could not have worked out better as many folk from Bunker Hill United

Methodist suddenly became very interested in helping the Armenians find milk powder."

Along with this chance visit, it so happens that the School of Christian Living event is scheduled for a couple of days later at Mount Tabor UMC in Winston-Salem, North Carolina. How fortuitous these four men show up right at this time, for Suzanne takes them with her to the *Christianity in the Communist World* class she is teaching. She explains why they are in the country, much less at this event, and what they need. Her introduction of them allows an unexpected opportunity to present the project to get milk for Armenia; the critical appeal sparks genuine interest as people immediately connect with the need. "By the time these chaps left America eight days later," Suzanne shares, "they had milk powder for the entire country as a result of the concerted effort of that class, the General Board of Global Missions, both North Carolina UMC Conferences, Bunker Hill United Methodist Church, several US aid organizations and with help from the Armenian Diaspora of Los Angeles."

Sandy Waldron is active in missions, locally and internationally, and typically attends every event she can to support mission projects. Having begun in 1986, she goes on an international mission trip at least once a year, and works on as many local mission projects as time allows. To her, church is not just a place to go on Sundays. It is a lifestyle. She practices what she preaches.

That is why the minister at Pine Grove has no qualms

about asking Sandy to drive the church bus to Mount Tabor UMC, also in Winston-Salem, for the School of Christian Living. He's fairly certain she already plans to attend the event. But because only three members of her congregation show up for this year's training session, she decides to drive her truck instead of the bus and stay for a course.

Held once a week for every week in February, the School of Christian Living is an annual event. This year's selection of classes offers something out of the ordinary. It is 1992 and the Soviet Union has just fallen, so when they arrive at Mount Tabor and Sandy sees a class on *Christianity in the Communist World,* she decides that is the one she wishes to attend. The class is taught by Suzanne Stafford and as she begins to speak, she introduces the four men who are visiting America to the class. It turns out that they are Armenian and they have literally, it seems, come out of nowhere.

As their story is shared, Sandy's mind wanders back to her childhood days. "Eat your food. The Armenian children are starving." She can still hear her father's voice saying those words with great regularity, for it was a familiar comment from people of his generation.

Everyone in the class is mesmerized by Suzanne's words, and excited that they are getting way more than they bargained for in attending this particular class. It is a day Sandy vows never to forget. She is immediately hooked on Armenia and what is happening in that small country as it recoils and has to rebuild itself from the ground up.

In later years, Sandy proudly claims, "I tell people I got to Armenia because I knew how to drive a bus." A light chuckle always accompanies her statement.

CHAPTER 4

When God Speaks

And suddenly there came a sound from heaven . . . Acts 2:2

Rev. Charles Davis sits in his den, dreading the evening's agenda. He is going to a District Missions Saturation Event. Not because he has any inclination to go, but because it is a mandate from his district superintendent. At the last ministers' meeting, the superintendent gives a reminder about the event, concluding with, "This year's district missions event will be at the Moore County Agriculture Center in Carthage. I *will* be taking names."

In the approximately 20 minutes it takes him to drive from his parsonage to the Moore County Agriculture

Center, in Carthage, NC, he thinks of possibly 20 small projects he can tackle with his growing collection of new woodworking tools once he reaches retirement. It isn't that Charles is against missions - quite the contrary. He has been extensively involved in missions during his ministry. In fact, he has served as the District Mission Coordinator of the Sanford District for a number of years, planning and organizing various mission events for the North Carolina Conference during his tenure in that position.

The typical format for this saturation event is to bring in different missionaries who are either on furlough in America, particularly the east coast, or who have recently retired. They are the speakers during the course of the three nights of sessions, each one making a presentation regarding the work with which he or she is involved. The subject for the day is to be something about Russia or the Soviet Union; at least that is Charles' impression as he attends the meeting with Jim Tatum, the pastor of the charge next to his.

A young woman, Dr. Suzanne Stafford, is the guest speaker for the evening. She immediately begins telling the group about the devastation and starvation in Armenia and how three calamitous events have set them into an unparalleled situation.

In Charles' words, "She shows up and starts painting this pitiful version of Armenia." He immediately connects with what she is saying, for he remembers his mother always saying, "Eat your food. The children of Armenia are starving." It is a term used often in his childhood, so he directs all his attention to what Suzanne has to say.

To hear Charles tell about it, "She had placed a large map on the wall, right in front of the long table where I was sitting. It was like it was staring straight at me. And as Suzanne is going on about Armenia, Jim leans over to me and asks, 'Where is Armenia?' I look back at him and answer, 'I don't know but I think it's in North Africa.'" In later years, he laughs loudly as he explains, "I was thinking about Algiers.

"She was going on and on and on and it sounded like the world was going to come to an end in Armenia and suck us all into it."

So as Charles sits there and hangs on Suzanne's every word, while staring at the large map on the wall, he hears a voice say to him, "Charles, I want you to go to Armenia." He knows immediately it is the voice of God, and stranger than that, it is as clear as Jim turning to him only moments before to ask the whereabouts of the country.

Charles quickly looks around the room, something like what he supposes one does should they see a flying saucer. "If you see a flying saucer, you certainly don't want to tell anybody. When God speaks to you openly, you do not go out and immediately announce it to the world." He makes up his mind not to say a word about what has just happened. But he does find Armenia on the map at that point.

Following the completion of the presentation, Charles moves toward the podium to catch Suzanne. He immediately introduces himself and says, "I want to help you. And I want to dedicate the rest of my life to helping you help Armenia. I feel like I've had a calling."

She, to this day, still remembers his words as distinctly as if he'd uttered them yesterday. She also remembers warning him that he may feel a bit differently come morning.

On the way home from the evening's mission event, Charles hears God speak again, saying the very same thing, "I want you to go to Armenia." His mind goes into a tailspin as he thinks through all the logistics of that command.

First of all, he reasons, *if I go to Armenia, it's going to have to be for more than a few weeks.* Having done a reasonable amount of mission work, he comes up with a three-month time frame to adequately assess the situation. He goes through all the many obstacles standing in his way. The first thing he is going to have to do is talk to his wife, Ann, when he gets home because he knows it has to get past her first. *Which isn't likely,* he realizes.

And then there's the Pastor-Parish Committee at the church. He knows they are not about to let the preacher be gone for three months. Not to mention he has a district superintendent that is going to say, "Charles, if I were you, I wouldn't talk about this much."

Lastly, there's a bishop who is going to look at him and say, "Charles, your name is on the moving list."

He gets home, aware that the first item on his agenda is to speak to Ann. Yet he has no idea how to pose the question of being gone that long to her. She's used to him going on mission trips, but usually for only two or three weeks at a time. Charles is up and down all night, until finally he can stand it no longer. He wakes her at five in the morning and with no prelude into the subject asks, "'Ann, how would you feel about me going to Armenia on a mission?"

Having heard him restless while up and down all night, she is already aware something is on his mind before the question hits the air. She says nothing for a minute or two, but in her heart, she knows this is something she has to let him do. So Ann answers simply, "Well, if you really want to."

When Charles shares this bit of the story with Suzanne and Sandy many years later, they both laugh. Sandy, in her quick wit, instantly responds, "Ann must have had a revelation too."

Ann's six words are all he needs. He is in his study within an hour writing letters for support to his family. Later that morning, he calls Suzanne. "This is the morning and I still intend to help you."

He calls for a meeting with the Pastor-Parish Committee, certain of the outcome. One dear lady says, "Well, Preacher, if God has asked you to do it, you'd better do it. It's a revelation."

The next step is to see the district superintendent. Charles describes exactly his proposal, expecting a negative reaction. But to his amazement, the superintendent replies, "It sounds to me like you've got something special going on in your life and I'll support you in any way I can."

At this point, there is no doubt in Charles' mind that God is in this, and that he has not mistaken the voice calling to him. Still, he knows the biggest obstacle is still to come . . . the bishop. So he schedules a meeting and visits the conference office. Pushing all of his qualms aside, he goes into the bishop's office and says precisely what is on his mind.

Without a moment's hesitation, the bishop immediately says, "I'm not going to get in the way of it!"

All the people he knows will stand in his way, yet no one does. Charles is elated but knows he has much work and research ahead of him before he can just take off to another country. *Especially one that only days before, I didn't even know where it was*, he admits to himself with a slight touch of humor.

On his way downstairs from the bishop's office to get a cup of coffee, Charles is spotted by a dear friend, Sam Dixon (Director of Missions for the North Carolina Conference of The United Methodist Church, and who later becomes the head of UMCOR - The United Methodist Committee on Relief). Sam, having already heard the news, jokingly yells down the stairs, "Charles, what did you do to upset God so badly?"

"Nothing," replies Charles.

"Well I smell trouble for you and me," Sam says with a friendly smile.

It is only then that Charles is at all scared. Everyone he expected to stand in the way of his going to Armenia approves. He never suspects that outcome. *Especially for it to be that simple*, he is quick to recognize, knowing it is all a part of God's handiwork.

Charles goes home and begins reading everything he can find on the history and culture of Armenia. The more he reads about the church, the more impressed he is that they have been practicing Christianity since 300 AD. He suddenly realizes he would feel ridiculous going over there and trying to tell them how to be Christian. They may have forgotten what they'd learned, due to being under Communist control for so long and banned from attending worship services, but he knows that Christianity is there. It's embedded in them.

So he makes up his mind from the get go, before he ever even leaves for Armenia, he will *not* attempt to make United Methodists out of them. He wants to see The United Methodist Church help the Armenian Apostolic Church get back on its feet. *I want us to help get its seminary going again and regain its strong vital leadership. I want to see it provide the strong leadership that God had originally intended for it.* But he is cognizant enough of the fact that this must happen through a humanitarian effort, for that is their mandate.

Charles contacts Suzanne and she sets up a meeting with him in Durham, North Carolina. They talk for a long while, going over all that is necessary to make his three-month assessment a reality. At the end of the extensive meeting she asks, "Are you going back home and forget this?"

He answers, "No, I think it's already gone too far." With that answer, Charles is quick to understand that the approvals are the easy part; now comes the real work. He will go to Armenia with no credentials from the conference or with any financial help from the conferences. Back in his study at home, he pens 76 letters and receives 75 replies back in return. (He later learns the other one has died, so that explains never receiving a response from that individual.) Every single one of the letters includes a pledge, thereby allowing Charles to raise approximately $4,000.00 to cover his expenses.

The call from God is not forgotten. The crate filled with all the new woodworking tools, still in the packaging, *is* forgotten.

PART Two

Infancy - Adolescence

First Steps - Growing Pains

CHAPTER 5

Up, Up and Away

Suzanne Stafford hears nothing else from Rev. Charles Davis until a few months later when a group meeting is scheduled for several interested parties who are committed to going on an assessment trip to Armenia. She wonders if he is still willing to go for the three-month period to thoroughly evaluate the country's situation. But when the day of the meeting arrives, so does Charles—money in hand, and ready to leave when the time comes.

Also at the meeting are Dr. Kyles Wallace— Suzanne's minister—along with a couple of other ministers, Rev. Bob Huffman (retired) and Rev. Elizabeth Forrest, from area UM churches. A few other interested individuals, Lori Bingham, Sarah Reynolds Dixon, Roger Duggins (who accompanied Kyles to Suzanne's house when the Armenians first arrived), and Sandy Waldron, a woman Suzanne recognizes from her earlier class at the School of Christian Living, are also in attendance. From that day she first encountered the four Armenian men in the class, Sandy's viewpoint is that this is a God-blessed project. For that reason, there is no doubt in her mind that God has called her to Armenia for this year's mission trip.

After much discussion, and a show of hands, it appears that each person seated at the meeting has heard the same voice as Charles, and is committed to going to Armenia for two weeks, via Moscow, to see about the possibilities of setting up a religious humanitarian aid project, and what the immediate needs of such a mission are. They are invited by the Apostolic Armenian Church, who is very excited about the prospect of re-establishing Christianity in this country, after their banishment from any kind of open worship or religious practices—save maybe the lighting of a candle in a sanctuary—during their communist tenure.

That is not the only invitation they receive. When the four Armenian men return to their homeland, they are so appreciative that they extend an invitation for the group of nine United Methodists to come to Armenia and see the situation with their own eyes. The group is to be hosted by the four men, two of whom are bankers and two of whom work at the Amalgamated Milk Factory in Yerevan.

So in October 1992, the original group of nine men and women fly together to Moscow, expecting to go straight on to Yerevan. They run into a slight hiccup, however, when they discover the difficulty of getting a flight from Moscow to Armenia, and later getting one back from Armenia to Moscow.

"You see, what happened," explains Charles later, "is when they dissolved the Soviet Union, the old communist crowd came and took all of the goods out of Armenia, all the aircraft and everything else and carried it back to Russia."

"Plus they were in war at that time," adds Sandy. "We could hear the scrapping and the bombing from the airport in Moscow." She laughs, something she was unable to do at the time this was actually happening. "The airline was having to wait for enough planes to come in to siphon enough fuel to send another plane back into Yerevan. So every morning we'd go to the airport early, and along about 10 or 11 o'clock they'd say, "There will be no plane to Armenia today. So we'd go back into Moscow and get a room again and go sightseeing or whatever."

Each night's room is at a different hotel so continual lugging of baggage is a part of their experience. It is a game to see if buses for the airport will run, or if a taxi is needed. The expenses of lodging, transportation and extra meals become an added surprise to their trip. On the back side of that coin, the sightseeing opportunities are beyond compare. Suzanne's expertise keeps them occupied and provides them with some memorable experiences.

For the second day in a row, breakfast is canceled. The nutrition bars the group has brought in case of an emergency get good use.

"Part of the camaraderie of the group," Suzanne

shares, "was finding enough to eat because this was a really hard time. Some man had flown in from Los Angeles with a whole bag of food from McDonald's. He was an immigration attorney and was going into Armenia to help them set up immigration laws. A representative of the president of Armenia was there to meet him. Remember that nice looking man in a trench coat?" she asks.

Sandy nods. "On the third day, they finally told us there would be a plane, but they didn't tell us what time so, of course, no one left the airport. By late afternoon, the Armenians who were also waiting for a plane were trying to share everything they had with us. So our group went out to the sidewalk kiosks and bought up a bunch of food and brought it back. We had a great big picnic right there in the lobby of the airport sharing with everybody."

Kyles, who has a wonderfully detailed journal of the account, says, "We purchased cheese, sausage, oranges, apples, cherries and orange Go-Go juice. Richard, the attorney, shared some of the cheeseburgers from McDonald's that he was taking to friends in Armenia. Other Armenians in the airport donated Sokolat chocolates for dessert. It was a regular gourmet meal!" There is a pause. "But then as we wait, the meal becomes like Holy Communion."

His words sending a startling, and at the same time deeply heart-warming, chill through the body. For the Armenians of the group, who have been denied religious freedom for so long, that is exactly what this is. And for the Americans who have known nothing like this lifestyle, it is a reminder of the life their Redeemer gave for them. That thought is reiterated by Kyles' next words. "The patience of the people awaiting the airplanes is representative of the virtue of God." His last words, "God is good," depicts the group's experience of perseverance in a way they'd never dreamed imaginable as they suddenly recognize and live those simple words of a child's first blessing.

"We also had a couple who were emissaries of the American Embassy waiting for the plane," adds Charles. "They were trying to get into Armenia too." The group finds a small, but meaningful, respite of comfort when this couple gives them the name of the American Consulate who handles American citizen's services in Armenia.

"There was an Armenian lady we met that day, Jasmine, who shared her heart's gratitude upon discovering our intended mission to her homeland. She had lived in London for 30 years, but was returning home to 'take something to my people.' Jasmine then wept as she managed, 'The whole world is cutting it off . . .'"

Suddenly, at 5:45 p.m., there is an announcement of a Yerevan flight. The group of nine is checked through security. They wait inside a holding room before moving to the tarmac in open weather. The temperature is below freezing and it is snowing as they walk to the plane, more than a half mile in the blowing snow. (Ironically, all the coach passengers are taken out to the plane on a bus. The first class passengers are the ones who have to walk.) When they finally reach the plane, it is full. Their attempt to board is futile. People without tickets have rushed the plane and covered the ramps, making it impossible for anyone to board.

From Kyles' journal: "The mad rush is subdued by

the police, as one of them uses his baton to both move and remove a number of stubborn passengers-to-be. Unruliness prevails, as police struggle to subdue it. Hopeful passengers scramble to the rear of the plane at approximately 6:30 p.m. as police check each boarding pass. Persons with no boarding pass are thrown to the tarmac off the ramp; there are 24 of them."

Charles adds, "Policemen went inside the plane, removed them and threw them down the steps. Right down in front of us. We asked, 'What's going on here?' but then realized that is how they were getting enough people off the plane to make room for those who had purchased tickets. A lot of people had bribed their way onto the plane."

"Yes," explains Suzanne, "they were Armenians from other countries whose ancestors had fled during the genocide. They were attempting to go help their 'brothers and sisters' in their native homeland, 'Sea to Sea' Armenia."

"Remember that little guy sent by the president to meet the attorney?" asks Sandy. "He walked down through the plane and asked, 'How many of you will give up your seats for the Americans?' And that is how we got our seats. Passengers were standing, sitting in the aisles, standing down the steps leading into the cargo hold, which was also full of people."

"Our group finally gets to board the plane after 2 ½ hours of standing in fuel on the tarmac," shares Kyles. "We are frozen. Flight crews are smoking under the plane, cigarettes hanging from their mouths as they too are standing in fuel and putting siphoned fuel in the plane . . . dangerous. Police with machine guns are tense. So are we.

"But then, with all the people standing in the aisles of Flight Ily 86, flight attendants corral all of the passengers, seated and standing, into the back of the plane. We learn this is necessary in order to distribute the weight so the nose gear will rise at takeoff. The gentleness and kindness of these attendants is moving beyond description. For a brief—very brief—moment, it erases the danger of the scenario from one's consciousness.

"And then, back to reality," he continues, "I wish many more people I know could be here. Although I am quite fearful, having never been in this type of situation before, I pray. 'For this is, yet, in the Name of God. So let it be done.' With the prayer, I sense a certain assurance."

Although Kyles is the minister and Suzanne is his parishioner, he notes an unbelievable strength in her, which he pens in his journal. "Stafford is a ROCK.'" He places the pen in his pocket after one last note . . . "We go."

"And what was it, 10 o'clock at night when we finally left?" asks Sandy.

"9:45," confirms Kyles, "for a 2 hour, 20 minute flight." He recalls the flight. "Some people were quiet, some slept. Faces exhibit unconcerned expressions, but return smiles. Children enjoy our snack crackers and breakfast bars, and also the orange drink Suzanne had purchased in the airport. We fly, struggling to believe this is all real."

"One side of the seat had a seatbelt, the other side didn't," recalls Charles.

"That's right," agrees Sandy.

Charles laughs as he tells what was not funny at the time. "I went to lean back in the seat and it didn't have a stop on it. I leaned back and all at once, I was looking in this guy's face behind me." The memory evokes spontaneous laughter from the entire group. "That's when I looked down at something on the floor and asked what it was. The guy beside me calmly answered, 'Hand grenades.'

"'What?' I asked in horror, to which he responded, 'Yes, look.' They were all under the seats, under the people's feet, along with all sorts of shells and ammunition."

"In the back of the plane it was totally full of boxes of hand grenades and ammo, plus the cargo hold was full of them too," interjects Sandy.

Charles, in his storytelling mode, says, "I looked at Kyles and asked, 'Kyles, have you got anything against cremation?' Kyles gives me an odd look as he inquires, 'What do you mean?'"

Jokingly, Charles replies, "If this thing goes up, man, we're going to be in about five countries." Then, in all seriousness, he adds, "You had to joke about it to keep from being scared out of your wits."

"At that point," says Sandy, "Kyles was getting a little nervous."

"He really was," agrees Charles, whose face suddenly exhibits the emotion they had all quietly experienced at that moment in time.

Sandy, in a very solemn tone, adds, "But you know, I think even with Kyles, that was the only time any one of us had any reservations through the entire trip. That plane trip was the only thing."

"It certainly was an unsettling moment, though," admits Suzanne, recapping the anxiety of getting off the ground after three longs days of waiting. "Before we could take off, what exactly did the pilot say?"

"Oh," recalls Charles, repeating nearly verbatim the "everybody go to the back of the plane."

"That's right!" exclaims Suzanne, briefly reliving the moment. "The aisles were full of people standing so he told them to all go to the back of the plane so he could get the nose off the ground. That's when someone told me, 'You'll be glad that a lot of these pilots are Russian fighter pilots. Whereas our US pilots had to have 2 years of training, their pilots had to have seven, so they're good.' And they were!"

"Yes, they were," seconds Sandy, "because when we got to Armenia, the runway had been bombed. We hadn't even started slowing down when we were about halfway down the runway and there were all these woods in front of us so he gets to the end of the runway and makes a U-turn, still in the air, and we went in again and finally got stopped."

"Everyone rejoices at the 'safe' landing," Kyles comments, recalling his relief of that moment.

"How many airports did we stop at on the way to Armenia?" asks Suzanne.

"I don't know," replies Sandy. "I slept all the way through."

"We had to stop at airports to get extra gas from other planes to get there and the plane get back to Moscow," Suzanne clarifies, "because Armenia wasn't rated high enough to get fuel. There was a big discrimination."

Kyles recalls those stops. "I saw Sochi long before there was any thought of the Olympics being held there.

We stopped there in the middle of the night, no lights inside or outside of the plane, to purchase pirated fuel. At first I had no idea what was going on as the plane descended and briefly stopped. You couldn't see a thing, save the light from the smokers outside filling the tank with enough gas to get us to Armenia and get the plane on its way back to Moscow. It was like something out of a movie. I'll never forget that as long as I live.

"Oddly enough, that plane ride was smooth as silk. But well it should have been with all that weight. We were certainly overweight for it was later confirmed that there were 500 passengers on board a 400-seat aircraft. There is no doubt that we flew by faith, so as we are saved." Kyles chuckles as he adds, "I well remember what Steve Siler, one of my Bunker Hill members said to me just days before we left, 'This trip may change your whole life.' Indeed, no truer words!

"I recall pondering, about the incidents prior to boarding, and the safety of the plane during flight, and coming to one conclusion: 'There is *no* safety here. There is no other way to do this, but by faith. No doubt, anything of uncertainty is related to a CONTROL issue. I am obviously powerless here—not to be confused with feeling powerful in other situations—but it was merely a feeling. But I fully grasped that in times like these, it is confirmed that there is never a time we do not live by faith."

"It was about 2 or 2:30 in the morning before we finally arrived in Armenia," admits Sandy, "and our hosts were standing there waiting for us with bottles of vodka. They had a big dinner waiting for us. They had slaughtered an animal, a goat or something, every day waiting for us to arrive. And when we didn't, they'd share it with their neighbors. At least we helped to keep the people fed," she concludes with a smile.

"I'll never forget the ride into the airport in Yerevan," Charles interjects. "They must have been doing 75 or 80 and all these policemen would step out and the driver would just keep going right on past them. We learned that the policemen weren't paid. The only way they could get any money was to get out in the street and bribe you. They'd take your license from you and take it down to a place where you could get it back in a week, and you'd have to go through all kind of hassles to get it back.

"Or you could pay a bribe and keep your license," adds Suzanne. "But it was their only way of income."

Needless to say, the turmoil of travel itself bonds these nine individuals into a strong foundation on which Project AGAPE can build and grow. It creates a reliance of faith to persons already deeply steeped in ministry and missions. And it prepares them for a world totally foreign to the realm of life to which they are all accustomed. It does not remove the shock of what they are about to encounter, but it shows them that in the midst of wars, struggles and poverty, there is an abundance of love and appreciation—and "Khaghaghut'yun" (peace)—that exudes from Armenia, the oldest Christian nation in the world.

The ride of that group should be appropriately labeled "The Remarkable 9." It begins a now 20-year-long journey, taking off into the wild blue yonder—a land of the unknown—and suffers many bumps along the way, some from an earthquake, some from the bombing, some from the fall of the Soviet empire; but all leading to the total collapse of Armenia's infrastructure. It has all the makings of an adventure movie; not one with all of Hollywood's chills and thrills, but with all the chills and thrills that come about only through God's amazing grace and unconditional love . . . love for **all** nations and **all** people. And it closes with an unforgettable ending, a story of an unmeasured outpouring of love and peace . . . AGAPE love that could only come from the Father who called them all to board that plane, Flight Ily 86 from Moscow. The final "amen" is the peace they learn, known to the Armenians in the word "Khaghaghut'yun."

As "the Remarkable 9" think back to that ride into the wild blue yonder, they all realize that the entire episode—riddled with humor that was anything but humorous at the time, and horror and disaster that was more than horrendous and disastrous at the time—still resonates within the hearts and minds of all who endured it. And when asked if they would do it again, the reply is always unanimously the same. "Yes!"

CHAPTER 6

On a Mission

In the few days they are in Armenia, the nine visitors from North Carolina witness firsthand the starvation, the destruction and the poverty that is present on every scene of this country. They also witness the remainders of "the way things were," with regards to the brilliance and intellect of the people. It is almost like they are in two worlds, which—in a manner of speaking—they are when one considers that a portion of what was once a part of their country is now disputed territory.

"When we visited the hospitals," describes Sandy, "because of the war effort, they had developed some state-of-the-art orthopedic appliances that had not been used anywhere else in the world."

"The appliances actually regrew bone," continues Charles. "But all of that was gone. Hospitals were closed. Schools were closed. They didn't have fuel, they didn't have food and they didn't have medicines. Because the government had collapsed, all of their law enforcements had been broken down. There was no money to pay anything." He pauses in a moment of reflection. "The people were brilliant, just brilliant. They had built much of the equipment for our space program. This place had it all." There is silence, obviously sparked by a pang of regret. "And they lost it all in the course of three cataclysmic events."

"Our hosts could not have been more gracious though," Sandy is quick to share, "whether it was a big dinner, or whatever else. They took such good care of us."

"Remember our visit to the milk factory where two of the Armenians who had come to visit me worked?" asks Suzanne.

Kyles certainly remembers that visit. Rev. Bob Huffman and he conduct the first United Methodist worship service ever on Armenian soul, and it takes place at the Amalgamated Milk Factory in Yerevan, Armenia. He still recalls verbatim the overwhelming awe he felt at that moment, especially as they served communion. His only word is "Wow!"

There is an immediate realization from the team that the entire country's infrastructure is broken. In fact, there is very little of any kind of structure left in the country at all except what is found in the Armenian Apostolic Church. That is the only structure that is actually holding the country together. They are excited about the possibilities of working together in a partnership to help re-establish Christianity in their country. Because of the change in the practice of religion during the communist years, there could be no formal training for seminary students. With the support of The United Methodist Church, textbooks, and all manner of supplies for the classroom study and dorm residence now become possibilities.

(An interesting point at this juncture is that Suzanne's resume landed in the headquarters of the General Board of Global Ministries on Riverside Drive in New York City. The offices of the Armenian Apostolic Church in America are housed in that same building that houses several interfaith agencies. In looking at the situation, it seems another example of God's hand at work.)

The problem with the infrastructure," explains Suzanne, "is their sudden absence of central planning. The small republics were used to everything happening from one center and reaching out to the countries. That was their mindset, and it had been for all those decades, so no one knew any different. They had never been faced with many of the decisions that were now essential to not only their development and growth, but their daily living and well-being, as well."

It becomes immediately obvious to the nine that much seed planting will have to be done, with the Americans and Armenians working together. The relationship between the two churches is a good "common denominator," of sorts. It allows The United Methodist Church good groundwork. Yet the needs for humanitarian aid are so prevalent that it will require a careful balance between helping the country find its own footing and helping the people simply to live, now that the three basic needs of food, shelter and clothing are no longer available.

It is going to be a difficult task, at best, to organize and develop a lasting and working relationship between the two countries. This is evident to all nine members of the team. But what is more evident is the fact that they are all aware of God's presence already in the project, and that is where they lay their confidence. They stand firm in the commitment to help this country whose condition cannot even be termed "in dire straits."

After a brief, but extensive, survey of the area, the group—now eight—returns home with pages of their initial findings, ready to move forward in partnership between The United Methodist Church and the Armenian Apostolic Church. Their flight, every bit as difficult as the first one, causes no problems for they are now prepared for any obstacles. Charles, who does not go back, is now ready to begin his three months of in-depth assessments.

Suzanne arranges for Charles to stay with a young family – a young man, his wife and their two children, a boy and a girl. The man serves as Charles' driver and interpreter around Armenia. It is with this family that he gets a fast and furious education, and a firsthand dose of the way things now are in this country, not to mention what he must endure over the course of the next three months. "For instance, let me tell you about refrigerators. When I stayed there for those first three months, I discovered that refrigerators were used to keep things from freezing in the winter. People would put food or something in them so it would not freeze because there was no electricity. You also have to understand that there was very little water and absolutely no heat. What people fail to understand is that when the Soviet Union fell, **everything** fell."

The first item on Charles' agenda is a visit to meet Archbishop Pargev Martirosyan (the head of the Diocese of the Armenian Apostolic Church of Artsakh). It is a profitable visit for both men, who immediately develop a great respect for each other. Pargev is also greatly respected by everyone in the republic and is known and admired by the soldiers who survived the recent war with Azerbaijan. That is because he was no stranger to the battlegrounds, for he would visit—even going to the front lines—to pray with soldiers and over the dying. This meeting lays much of the groundwork for not only these three months, but for the later years that Charles will spend in Armenia. More importantly, it becomes a common bond between these two men for all of the future humanitarian work there.

In his three months, he travels most all of Armenia. Everywhere he goes, the vision is the same – all of the factories have been closed. "It was hard to believe," Charles describes sorrowfully, "for we are talking like rocket scientists . . . literally! They were significantly involved in the space program. The Armenians were, and still are, highly intelligent."

This goes back to the sudden absence of the central planning Suzanne mentioned. "One of the first things I did," explains Charles, "was to visit the few hospitals still trying to provide care, for most all of them had closed like the factories. There were no supplies, medicines . . . nothing for them to use to help or comfort the patients. As I would speak to the doctor at each facility regarding their situation, I would get the same response. 'Our money hasn't come from the Central Committee.' And I would try to explain, 'Look, your money's no longer *going* to come from Central Committee. That money is gone.' It was so sad . . . they had it, and lost it." Charles' expression matches his words. "Communism was no more. They may have changed their name, but they did not change their ways. They knew no other way. For many of the residents, communism was all they had ever known."

In the three months Charles is there, he travels even into the occupied portion of the country. As the group of nine has already assessed, he continues to see throughout the whole of the territory that the most immediate needs are clothing, food and medicine. He makes detailed notes of each place, what the possibilities are, what other areas of humanitarian aid are necessary and how the churches at home can go about meeting those various needs.

When December of 1992 arrives and his plane leaves for America, Charles knows his work is not done. He is determined to help Armenia and its people, and he understands that God will work out all of those details. He prays and waits for the next move of God's hand.

CHAPTER 7

It's Official

One of Charles' first obligations, once he returns to the States, is to meet with his bishop and several other groups in the Raleigh, North Carolina area. As he describes the needs and the plan he envisions for developing and growing a project in Armenia and the disputed territory with each audience, he makes sure two points are clear from the outset. This is not a mission about going over there and trying to convert the Armenians into United Methodists. There is no need; the churches and the Christian spirit are still there, despite everything done during the Stalin regime to destroy them. Rather, instead of simply finding a sanctuary and lighting a candle for loved ones, a fire needs to be rekindled within the faith to re-establish the Armenian Apostolic Church in order to help them again fill up their seminaries and bring Christian education back into the schematics of the country's new way of thinking.

When annual conference time rolls around in June for both the North Carolina and Western North Carolina Conferences, Charles is invited to speak. He receives full support of both conferences as they, together, prepare to enter into a religious humanitarian aid project and send him back to Armenia to serve as the Executive Director. Financial support will come from both conferences to begin the effort and get it off the ground. Given the obstacles he has already endured on getting off the ground from Moscow to Yerevan, and then again from Yerevan to Moscow on his first trip, Charles is somewhat equipped for perils that may arise.

He immediately begins seeking the support of his family to help with Project AGAPE, as it is now formally and appropriately called. Fortunately three of Charles' brothers are pharmacists and are dedicated to helping him acquire medicines through their connections with the drug companies. Their efforts allow him to take two suitcases filled with medicines on his return trip. A recent flood in Armenia causes continual outbreaks of all sorts of diseases, so the medicines are well received by the hospitals and clinics that have nothing. Charles wastes no time in setting up the purchase of medicines, supplies and some equipment to be shipped to Armenia in huge containers.

In February of 1994, the first Project AGAPE "team" comes to help and bring assistance when Dr. Bill Simpson and Dr. Sam Dixon arrive with 16 lockers filled with badly needed medicines and medical supplies. While surrounded by the sights and sounds of war-torn Nagorno-Karabakh, and witnessing the republic's needs first-hand, the three agree that the areas requiring the first and foremost assistance are unquestionably food, clothing and shelter, and long-term medical and educational support.

With a list from Charles' earlier three-month assessment period of 1992, Archbishop Pargev and Archbishop Nerses Pozapalian (the Archbishop of the Mother See of Holy Echmiadzin), offer a list of the most necessary items as their seminaries strive to increase enrollment and educate their priests. Project AGAPE helps by providing those requested materials of mimeograph machines, printers and computers. As churches again become active, Bible is taught in schools, Sunday School teachers are receiving training and Sunday School literature is being produced.

"The priests would come in from the villages and tell what their needs were once a month," states Charles. "That is how we made our strong connection with the Armenian Apostolic Church. It was in trying to help them get one of their seminaries reopened that had been closed during the low number of seminarians."

There may be no food and no heat here, but there is a huge desire to again become active in the Christian faith as Armenian souls are fed and hearts are warmed. The success of the partnership between The United Methodist Church and the Armenian Apostolic Church is evident when a later assessment of the seminaries shows a growth in enrollment from 26 students in 1993, to 256 students in 1995.

After suffering approximately 70 years of "spiritual oppression," it is enlightening to realize that through the assistance of Project AGAPE, the church of the oldest Christian nation in the world has moved from its oppressed state of being "the church of the clergy, for the clergy, by the clergy" to taking huge steps forward to once again become a "church of the people."

Charles soon learns that one of the difficulties of being in a former Soviet country is receiving shipments from America, as this had all been previously handled by the Soviet government. The Armenians, having no experience with a customs clearance office, have to completely restructure the entire process. As for the language barrier involved in his work, he admits, "I managed to get an Armenian keyboard and I went to the American University to recruit some of those students to work on my staff. That is where Nara Melkonyan (who is now the Country Director for Project AGAPE) worked when I hired her two years later.

"I was indeed fortunate to have a good staff. The fact that they were all Armenian was a huge part of our success. Even though our AGAPE office was in Yerevan, which also served as my housing, our field work could be 10 hours out of the city. Mardakert, which was as far out as we went, was about 10 hours away. That is where our field hospital was. We helped a lot of men there. The biggest problem of getting to Mardakert, and the other areas in the war zone, was finding someone to take me there. No one would dare drive into Nagorno-Karabakh. I happened to hear about a man, Hakob Gumbalyan, who had served in the military and currently worked at the World Council of Churches. I contacted him immediately to see if he would be willing to help me get medicine and medical supplies to the field hospital in Mardakert. Thankfully he agreed." (Hakob Gumbalyan is immediately hired by Project AGAPE after that and today, in addition to his role as a driver, is also their Director of Operations)

There is then silence as Charles thinks back to those former days. "One thing I always tried to tell people was to **never make promises,** which is the first rule of mission work, or work with any project. Too many people had come into Armenia, promised to help and then left without another word ever being heard from them. That needs to be emphasized to anybody who goes over there, or anywhere, on a team. Do not make any promises. I made sure I **never** did that."

He shakes his head. "But there is this one day that I remember going to Echmiadzin to visit the Catholicos. He told me about a special hospital they had out in Karabakh for children.

"'Father Charles,' he said, 'I've made a promise that I am afraid I cannot keep. I've promised the hospital 50 beds and I have no way of getting them.'

"I remember the look of desperation on his face, and the sadness in his voice, and the next thing I remember is saying, without thinking, 'I think I can get you the 50 beds.'

"I walked out of that place scolding myself for letting those words escape my mouth, and praying frantically that God would somehow intervene and help me find the beds. A couple of nights later I received a phone call from a man who was the director of a retirement home in Southern Pines, North Carolina. You'll notice that I always got **all** of my phone calls in the middle of the night because of the time change. But this man called and said, out of the clear blue, 'Charles, we've just done a remodeling job. I'm out in the warehouse and I've got a hundred hospital beds. Can you use any of them?'

"I immediately answered, 'I can use all of them, please!'"

"God's hand," interjects Sandy, repeating the two words that seem to be synonymous with "Project AGAPE" from its first seed of thought.

"That's the way things kept happening," admits Charles. "It would scare me sometimes. One thing I came to realize was that I didn't have charge of anything over there. The Lord had charge of it. I was just running to keep up."

Charles' four years of service in Armenia provide countless tons of blankets, medicine and medical supplies, clothing, shoes and socks, food . . . the list goes on and on. But more than that, the immeasurable energy and the innumerable relationships he made serve as the foundation of all the work that has gone on since the day of that plane ride of "The Remarkable 9."

Suzanne Stafford, in a meeting with Charles Davis and Sandy Waldron shortly before the release of this book, speaks of the many accomplishments of Charles during his time of leadership with Project AGAPE. She sums up her thoughts in one basic word. "It's phenomenal, Charles, what you did. Just phenomenal!"

When asked to what she credits the successful beginning of Project AGAPE, Suzanne loses no time in answering, "That first group over there; they were such wonderful diplomats. To my mind and dying day, I believe their energy helped Charles see and be enthusiastic about what could be done, because this was also his first time to see the country and the circumstances. Charles took their vision and their encouragement, and with his smarts and brilliance, managed to deliver. He made all the right decisions and took all the right courses. I flew over there three or four times and Charles was always off and gone helping people. It was so rewarding."

A benchmark comes for Project AGAPE in 1997. Originally planned as a 4-year project, it becomes evident that it needs to be an ongoing project and that much is still being accomplished in Nagorno-Karabakh. It is then formally incorporated in the state of North Carolina on June 5, 1997. From that, and from the success of the project in its subsequent years—under Nara Melkonyan's amazing leadership and the continued partnership between The United Methodist Church and the Armenian Apostolic Church—it seems a thumbs-up is in order for a "Mission Accomplished," at least as far as its beginnings and early stages. It has now advanced into the realm of "Ongoing Project" as hopefully more United Methodist conferences, as well ecumenical groups, will join the support so greatly needed for this area of the world that, in the midst of its endurance of countless struggles and hardships since ancient times, is oftentimes forgotten by the rest of the world.

CHAPTER 8

Coats Aplenty

First and foremost, after Charles gets settled in his new office facility and begins his position as the Executive Director of Project AGAPE, is to find a way to help the people of Nagorno-Karabakh survive the cold winter. At the suggestion of UMCOR (United Methodist Committee on Relief), a massive coat drive is launched for the people of Armenia and coats come in from all over America, as well as other parts of the world, in their relief effort. The call goes out for coats for men, women and children. Thousands upon thousands of coats are collected as people generously respond to the need. The coats—planned to arrive in the fall and be distributed to the Nagorno-Karabakh citizens by Charles prior to winter—run into a major glitch with the mountain of paperwork that must be completed for humanitarian aid to Armenia to be exempt from duties, tariffs and airport fees. It is a terribly cumbersome process, but everything is finally in order by the end of January.

Day in and day out, Charles anxiously awaits the coats he is to deliver. This is going to be a gargantuan project, and now because of the numerous hang-ups with the delivery along the way, even before this latest delay with all the paperwork, he wonders how he will ever get the coats to all the citizens before winter's end.

Finally, on the Saturday of February 12, 1994, in the worst snow storm of the year, he receives a call that the coats are finally on their way to Yerevan. He heads for the airport . . . and waits. At 8:00 p.m., the largest aircraft that was in the former Soviet fleet arrives with 118 tons of coats. It is dark. The temperature is 5 degrees above zero. And it is a weekend. But none of that matters now. The coats are here, and AGAPE is ready!

By 7:00 a.m. on Sunday morning, there are 130,000 coats in the AGAPE warehouse, all of them tied up in bundles like huge bales of cotton. Come Monday morning, trucks begin moving these "bales" of coats—provided for all the areas of Armenia and for Nagorno-Karabakh, which is still under fire—to their various appointed distribution points. In Charles' report, he writes: "Often times the coats were distributed under a barrage of rocket fire. In the Berd and Noyemberian regions, the distribution points actually are used as targets for rocket fire. While there were people wounded, fortunately there were no deaths and the coats were all distributed within 30 days of arriving at the airport in Yerevan."

Even though these deliveries happen under perilous wartime conditions, and over treacherous roads that are impassible even in the best of weather, they all arrive to their appointed destinations. The worst mishap is that several of the trucks are stuck in the hazardous mountain passes for five days . . . which could actually be a blessing. They finally arrive back with not a scratch on any of them.

Other coats have to be delivered to the people in Berdzor and the other areas of Kashatagh, including the many villages. Many of these areas, too, are entrapped in snow, making it nearly impossible for Charles to maneuver the Niva car to the places where coats are to go. Still, he perseveres, determined to have all the coats in the hands—and on the backs—of the thousands of Armenians looking forward to even the smallest respite from the bitter winter's cold. Recipients of the coats share the same sentiment, "Charles, in the dead of winter, endured the cold snowy weather and traveled over roads impassable to deliver the coats gathered from United Methodists all across the United States."

Some of the coats have notes in the pockets. Charles takes the time to read each note to its coat's recipient that he personally distributes. There is no wonder that the first coat he pulls from a "bale" to distribute is from North Carolina. Again, God's hand.

Accolades from grateful mothers, whose husbands and/or sons are off in the war, abound with their sincere appreciation of the effort that "Father Charles" makes in getting the coats to each and every one of their family members. Because of the weather and the road situations, it is well into the spring before some of the coats reach their final destinations. Although it may be a little late for the winter just passed, in 1993, everyone will have coats for the winter of 1994.

There is one particularly interesting observation from a man regarding the massive coat drive. His words sum up the feeling of what most everyone who encounters Rev. Charles Davis during his work with Project AGAPE says, "Many people come and talk to us and then go away. We never hear from them again. But Father Charles is different. He stays with us. He cares for us."

CHAPTER 9

A True Ambassador

Nara Melkonyan sits in her office at the American University of Armenia (an affiliate of the University of California), where she is the Admissions Director. Having worked in the office as a student at the school while she received her undergraduate degree and later her Master's degree in the area of Political Science and International Affairs, she is such an astute individual, hard worker and "people person" that they kept her. However, Nara's ambition is to be an ambassador and after four years of being in this position, she is ready to move on toward that career. In fact, to help her in that direction, she currently has an application in process with the USAID (United States Agency of International Development) for the position of Administrative Assistant and is awaiting a reply.

That is where her thoughts are when a visitor enters her office. This isn't just any visitor. It happens to be her cousin's brother-in-law who, being an attorney, helped Rev. Charles Davis to register Project AGAPE in Armenia in 1994. It also isn't his first visit to Nara's office. He has been here on a few occasions previously to get copies of court cases because his office has no copier. Each of those visits also includes a question.

"Would you be interested in working with a humanitarian aid agency, Nara? Project AGAPE is seeking a Deputy Director and you'd be great at the job."

Her response is always the same – a polite "no."

On this particular day in 1997, he has a request for her to type and print some court cases he needs. The request is accompanied by the same question.

This time, however, her answer is more than a word. "At the moment, I have an application in with the USAID as their Administrative Assistant and I should be hearing back from them any day now. You know I want to be an ambassador and this will help me move in that direction."

On his next visit, the attorney also brings his wife and Nara's cousin to her office to make copies. Since they all live in the same multi-apartment building, the trio offers to take Nara home when she finishes the needed copies. Only instead of taking her home, they "kidnap" her and take her to the AGAPE office to meet with Rev. Charles Davis. Nara, even though she is extremely upset—even to the point of being mad—refuses to allow her feelings to show and is her usual polite and congenial self.

When asked by Rev. Davis about the position, she answers simply, "I have other career goals." Yet her cousin, the attorney and his wife continue to persuade her to at least interview for the position. It isn't until Nara overhears one of the other AGAPE staff members tell the attorney's wife that "Rev. Davis has interviewed nearly 25 applicants and has not liked any of them" that she recalls one of the questions she was asked on the way here.

"Why don't you just try and see what happens? Just for interest? This can be a good experience for you." Her cousin's words from earlier play back through her mind.

That's right, Nara thinks when she considers the situation. *It can be good interview practice for me and I can't lose anything.* Still expecting to wait for other opportunities to arise, she agrees to at least speak with Rev. Davis.

"Rev. Davis asked me several questions and then accepted me immediately, telling me he would like me to work as the office director for AGAPE," Nara now admits. "It all happened so fast that the next thing I remember was the look of amazement on his face when I responded, 'I am sorry, but I need a probation period.'

"He was shocked for that is typically what an employer tells a new employee, but here I was giving him that ultimatum. Rev. Davis agreed, though, and I used my two-week vacation from the university for my probationary time at AGAPE. During that two weeks, I liked what I learned about the activities of the project, especially how they were helping the people who were suffering due to the war with Azerbaijan and the earthquake.

"And it actually did fit my character," she admits, "for I had been known by the students at the university as being someone who was ready to help them when they needed help. I remember one particular student from the Engineering department who needed help in fixing a broken small floppy disk. He was elated that I took the time to help him, yet it was such a menial task.

"The only reason I share this is because, after that two-week probationary period, I suddenly realized all the instances of times I had helped students at the university was out of the scope of my direct responsibilities. I truly loved helping people and I would certainly get to do that regularly if I accepted this position." She smiles. "Later, after I ran into one of the university students who learned I was working at AGAPE, he told me, 'You found a place fitting your nature.'"

But the story doesn't end there. During the course of Nara's probationary period, she receives a letter from the USAID stating that "you are overqualified for the position for which you have applied, but we would like to consider you for other positions fitting your qualifications."

"I actually did receive a call from them later," she explains. "'We would like to inform you that we have a suitable vacancy for you,' were their words. My answer to them was 'I am sorry, but I have found a job that I like.'"

Nowadays when Nara speaks of this experience, the story is accompanied by a laugh, not the anger she felt when she was "kidnapped." "I still do not understand, even after all this time, how it happened that I began working at AGAPE."

However, her expression says something else. Nara's infectious smile shows that she now understands it wasn't her cousin, her cousin's brother-in-law or his wife who were responsible for her interview and then acceptance of the position with Project AGAPE. "It was God's hand at work," she states humbly. And then as a footnote, she adds, "Looking back now, after my 17-year path of being here, I am confident in one thing. I will never regret it."

Anyone who watches Nara work—whether behind her desk, taking care of business (such as that at the customs clearance office), unloading the shipments, overseeing mission teams, distributing the Christmas shoeboxes or other items needed by families, the schools, the orphanage or Christian Education Center, or acting as the administrator and meeting with officials—can easily assess that she is indeed where she is supposed to be, doing exactly what she is supposed to be doing.

Some individuals are born to serve, some to get things done. Nara meets both qualifications and more. One can clearly understand how it is she controlled her emotions during her "kidnapped" episode and the interview with Charles Davis. Her professionalism, combined with a rare and innate concern for individuals, shines through in every aspect of her work. Her beautiful almond-shaped eyes and dark hair—so distinctly Armenian—are overshadowed even by her ever-pleasant demeanor and joyous smile that makes you happy simply to be in her presence. Her amiable disposition masks her emotions so that, no matter when you see her, she is always the same. Exhibiting a warm heart and caring spirit, it seems Nara is born for this position. She is amazingly wise in getting the most with the very limited resources she has available and sensitive in dealing with the needs of the people. Though ever ready to reach out to one in need, she possesses an astutely keen sense of discernment when it comes to weighing which family's hardship makes them most qualified as a recipient of the Cattle Project, either as new cows are purchased or cows already in the program are ready to be passed along to another family.

To understand the full impact Nara has on the lives of the residents of Berdzor and the outlying villages, one needs merely to walk with her down the mountain path from the AGAPE office to the streets of the town below. Besides being a delightfully meaningful experience, it is a treasured and valuable lesson.

Although everyone recognizes her, it is not an immediate reaction for most of those she passes on the street. It is rather amusing to see them nod at her and then their faces do a double-take when they realize who she is. The townspeople and villagers are so accustomed to seeing her only behind the desk of her office, or handing out shoeboxes or donations at the distribution center, they are pleasantly shocked to meet her out of her element. Everyone rushes to greet her, and once the children spy her, you are not sure whether the effect is more like the Pied Piper or Maria von Trapp, but either way, Nara is followed by an array of children.

Most of the adults are anxious to share news with

her, whether that means how well they are doing with things they have been given, or to make her aware of some great need from their family. For others, it is a chance to inform her they are ready to pass on a calf that has been born of the cow they received two or three years prior.

For one particular woman, it means an opportunity for a private hearing for her case of needing a cow from the Cattle Project. She is the mother of nine children and desperately needs the milk for her family. Nara informs her to come to the office and fill out an application. As the woman thanks her and walks away, Nara explains that there are many applicants, but only five cows this year to give. "However, this woman is a good candidate for a cow," she states. "She can provide many things for her family with the milk and its byproducts. Narrowing down the many families who are neediest will be most difficult over the next three weeks, at which time we will buy the five new cows for the recipients."

The most valuable lesson of the walk comes when Nara is asked how many people actually live within the town and the nearby area. She estimates 3,000 – 4,000. "I used to know exactly how many were here, for we helped everyone. Now we are only able to help 300 families, with approximately four per family, so I only know those for sure."

What her comment unspokenly admits is that people here are taking the assistance they have received and are using their resources and creative minds to improve their situations. Thus, they do not suffer the "revolving door" syndrome seen so much in America. It is most impressive that this society, though in dire need, is not "standing with their hands out," as the expression goes. It is refreshing to see firsthand that, in regards to weighing the needy vs. the greedy, Project AGAPE is a finely-tuned instrument, thanks greatly to Nara's wealth of knowledge of the people and her country, with the help of her staff. Together, their operation runs very smoothly, with seemingly no weak links.

One other notable lesson gleaned is the obvious trust and respect she holds from the people of Nagorno-Karabakh, whether the city officials, the poor and needy, the Archbishop of the Diocese of Artsakh, or the Consul of the Nagorno-Karabakh Republic in acquiring Visas for visitors and workers to the disputed territory. She is known throughout the republic and her work is deeply appreciated by all.

For those who know this extraordinary woman, especially ones who have worked alongside her either as a staff member or mission team member of Project AGAPE, one thing is for certain. Nara Melkonyan's dream of being an ambassador is now an actuality. Her role as the Armenia Country Director of Nagorno-Karabakh, not to mention her outstanding works, make her an ambassador in every sense of the word.

CHAPTER 10

Changing Seasons

There is a saying that "Without change, things cannot grow." Project AGAPE, like other organizations, experiences changes and transition. With the retirement of Rev. Charles Davis in September 1997 and the incorporation of Project AGAPE and its appointed Board of Directors—as well as changing needs with ongoing developments in Armenia still stemming from the fall of the Soviet Union and the war over Nagorno-Karabakh—there is a season of change. One of the greatest needs is to find a proper replacement for Charles. It is a joint decision between all parties involved that a Country Director for Armenia should be appointed, someone who is from Armenia and knows

78

the country (including the history, the people, the language and the culture), The Board of Directors can then act on recommendations from this person. Nara Melkonyan is named the Acting Director during this interim time.

As the Board of Directors seeks to grow and expand the project's work in Armenia, particularly in the Nagorno-Karabakh republic, this transition period proves to be the perfect time to examine the future of Project AGAPE and map out directions of change and growth. One of the desires of the board is to become more involved in the area of education, making it one of the main priorities for AGAPE. In order to facilitate what needs to happen, board members Rev. Alec Alvord and Darwyn Van Gorp (a retired Boy Scouts of America executive)—and his wife, Jeannine—travel to Armenia in March of 1998. Alec (Missions Secretary for the Western North Carolina Conference of The United Methodist Church) is to stay approximately ten days to check on things and to introduce Darwyn and Jeannine to Armenia and the Project AGAPE staff. Darwyn and Jeannine are to serve as co-directors of the project for 3 ½ months during this transition period. This will allow them to not only discover necessary changes and new goals, but actually implement some of them and see them through. By June, when they are to return home, they will have a detailed account of their findings to present during the Annual Report to the two North Carolina conferences.

Alec's first assignment is to introduce the Van Gorps to Nara Melkonyan and the AGAPE staff, one of whom is Hakob Gumbalyan. These two individuals, both strong leaders, are responsible for the work of the project during the interim time of Charles' retirement and the appointment of a Country Director to run Project AGAPE. Alec's next assignment is to show the visiting couple the projects already completed or in progress. With Hakob as their driver and Nara as their guide, he wastes no time in taking the Van Gorps to Spitak, the town worst hit by the earthquake of 1988 and still suffering desperately with their conditions for education.

Another journey takes them to two villages, Yervandashat and Bagaran, both on the Turkish border. Charles has previously helped Yervandashat get water, but the other village—Bagaran—does not have a whole water system. The women and children of Bagaran have to walk 2 - 3 miles to get potable water. There is a reservoir with a plentiful water supply up the mountain from the village.

Darwyn shares this story. "The mayors of those two villages so badly wanted water piped into their villages, that they were on my doorstep nearly once a week during the entire time I was at the Yerevan office." Considering this is a 70-mile trip each way, this is no easy task for the village mayors. Darwyn promises to see if there is anything that can be done for them once he returns to the States.

Upon his return, with the board's recommendation, the Western North Carolina Conference votes to support the water project. Yervandashat receives the help they need to complete their system. Darwyn is able to find the necessary pipe needed for Bagaran for $1,500.00, an excellent price for the amount needed to get the water from the reservoir down the mountain to the village. The conference then raises $20,000.00 to purchase the pump. Villagers are told they will have to do the work, which they do gladly. On the day the water is first pumped into the village from nearly three miles away, men stand at the pump splashing water on their faces and cheering loudly. Their faces show, without words, the joy brought to them by this dream come true. In times like this, there is no language barrier. Life for the residents of both villages changes immediately and dramatically, thanks to the love and support shown through Project AGAPE.

When questioned about the greatest needs he encounters and his most worthwhile accomplishment during the time his wife and he serve as interim Co-Directors of Project AGAPE, Darwyn loses no time in offering answers. "The greatest needs were simply the daily necessities of food, clothing and shelter. There was such a demand for warm winter clothing. Whole families, extended families, were living in whatever shelter they could find with only a covering over it. They also needed medicine and medical supplies, which relates to the most significant thing that happened while we were there.

"One of our first jobs there after Alec left was to check the AGAPE warehouse and see what was in it to determine what was most needed. We found it was packed full of medicine and medical supplies that had just been sent the month before to be distributed to 15 different villages, selected by the country's Minister of Health. The problem was that the village 'clinics' proved to be no more than first aid stations and no one in any of the village stations had any type of medical training or was equipped to use the medical supplies. A doctor in Yerevan was hired temporarily to help with this project and divide the medicines and supplies in the warehouse into 15 boxes, depending on each village's needs. He then took a small group with him to train the people at the village 'clinics,' where conditions were found to be deplorable. Jeannine was both humbled and gratified to be a part of the group that helped with this experience, which also provided food and transportation for those who participated in the training. Without the transportation, some of the participants would have had to walk 15 – 20 miles."

One of the villages, Sarshen,boasts a population of over 1,000 prior to the war but now has only 35 persons remaining. Another village, Tsamtsor, also has approximately the same number of inhabitants before the war and now there are only 60. The program turns out to be most beneficial for the village "clinics," as well as the people of the villages.

"We asked for people in the States to send used versions of the *Physicians' Desk Reference*, no older than two or three years old," states Darwyn, "so that nurses could find and recognize the various medicines and have the knowledge to give the right ones and the right doses. During the spring of 1998, we were able to offer and complete the training for the villages of Karabakh, equip the 'first aid stations' with medicines, and open the clinics.

"Our biggest problem while there was in helping both the school in Spitak and the village of Bagaran to get their shipping containers through customs," Darwyn admits. "There were around 12 or 13 offices involved, and all of them had to put their stamp of approval on everything.

All of the equipment and materials finally arrived, but it took a tremendous amount of time. As if that was not bad enough, we learned the week before we left about the lengthy delays in receiving all humanitarian supplies."

Two days before the Van Gorps are to depart from Armenia, Jeannine pens a letter to the President of Armenia, explaining that Project AGAPE is a program of North Carolina and The United Methodist Church and they receive *no* governmental funds. She pleads her case about why it is so extremely imperative that the shipments for Nagorno-Karabakh are allowed into the country in a timely fashion and how crucial the work of the project is to the disputed territory's people, their villages and their hospitals. Within days, Nara is invited for a private audience with the president.

Darwyn, in later speaking about this episode, chuckles and adds, "Nara had all the governmental contacts and knew that place inside and out." She speaks at great length with the president about the customs delays and when she leaves his office, everything is handled and many of the restrictions are dropped. The president's decision, thanks to Jeannine Van Gorp's letter of request—and Nara's intellect and tenacity—proves to be an incredible timesaver in claiming all future shipments.

At the recommendation of the Van Gorps, after they return to America, the Board of Directors votes unanimously to appoint Nara Melkonyan the Country Director for Project AGAPE. It is decided that, in the beginning phase of a new Country Director, a board member should travel to Armenia once a quarter to answer any questions and see if there are any problems or issues that require the board's input. This responsibility typically falls on Alec because of his position. But it is quickly learned that Nara is so adept at her job and proficient in email that all matters can be handled without the quarterly trips. She keeps immaculate records, detailed to the penny, and Hakob assists her in whatever way necessary.

"Without change, things cannot grow." During its 20-year history, Project AGAPE encounters many changes, all of which allow them to grow significantly in the many areas in which they serve. At the outset of the project, when it receives its State Registration in Armenia in 1994, there are some skeptics who give it five years. Now after 20 years, it is not only still in operation, but stronger and continuing to help more and more people in many different ways. They now receive ecumenical support from other groups and denominations, allowing them to continue to work as the *only* humanitarian aid project able to get into Nagorno-Karabakh.

PART THREE

Adulthood

The Working Years

CHAPTER 11

And the Earth Shook

The cold Wednesday morning starts as any other wintry day in Spitak on December 7, 1988. And then, at 11:41 a.m., the earth begins to shake, buildings crumble to the ground as if they are no more than a child's set of building blocks, and lives—large numbers of lives, 4003 in this town alone— are lost as the epicenter of a huge earthquake literally rips through the town of Spitak. In the short span of three seconds, two separate events happen that kill at least 25,000 people (40,000 by some counts), injures 19,000 and leaves half a million homeless in the Leninakin-Spitak-Kirovakan area of northern Armenia, at that time still part of the USSR. It measures 6.8 in magnitude and X for the damage measure, denoting devastation. The quake affects more than 20 towns and 342 villages, 58 of which are completely destroyed.

Landslides bury the railroad tracks. Power lines are majorly damaged. The area that is worst shaken is highly industrial; it houses chemical plants, electrical substations and power plants. The Metsamor Nuclear Power Plant is located only 47 miles from Spitak's epicenter. Although no actual damage occurs to the plant, it is closed for a period of six years for fear of another quake and does not reopen until 1995.

Most of the area's hospitals are destroyed and more than two-thirds of the doctors and medical staff are killed. This complicates the already-tragic situation immensely since there is now no way to care for the injured. All ten schools in the Spitak area are destroyed.

There is no family left without feeling its effect and the loss of loved ones. Life as Spitak knows it, for those who miraculously survive the quake, is gone forever. The situation is so bad that, for the first time since World War II, the frictions of the Cold War are laid aside when Soviet leader Mikhail Gorbachev formally requests humanitarian help from the United States—something else crumbled by the powerful earthquake.

Ten years after the earthquake, while Rev. Alec Alvord, Darwyn and Jeannine Van Gorp are in Armenia to do the assessment study, they seek ways for Project AGAPE to become more involved in the educational realm of the country. Although there has been some work with education since the project's official state registration in 1994, a large majority of the help has been with medicine. Thus the Board of Directors for Project AGAPE wishes to expand their educational efforts. Because of this and the dire need for help with schools still in Spitak, Nara takes them to this area.

The assessment team is greeted by hundreds of tombstones that dot the hilly landscape where once homes, factories and businesses stood. Most of the tombstones bear an etched portrait of persons killed. Some may have only one person's images; others have an entire family. There are some, in addition to family members, that have an etched carnation with a broken stem. Those symbolize the unborn child of a mother, also lost in the earthquake.

From that scene, they visit the schools, where they find the situations surrounding them to be heart-rending at best. Nearly 3,000 students are cramped into the temporary facilities erected following the earthquake. Most of the schools have no heat at all, and if they do have heat, the classrooms are filled with smoke and unhealthy fumes. One of the schools, School #7, is nothing more than classrooms constructed from converted shipping containers that have been sent to Armenia from around the world. Each classroom is one of those containers, with a hallway built between the containers to connect them.

What heat there is comes from a tiny heater in the middle of the classroom. Smoke is so thick and black from the heater that the teacher is unable to see the back of the classroom and students can barely see from one to the other. This is the largest school of the area, serving 450 students. Alec, Darwyn and Jeannine are so moved by the abysmal conditions of the school that they immediately propose a construction project for a new school to replace School #7.

Nara also takes them to meet Mayor Suren Avetissian—only 35 years old—whom they discover seems to be "just what the doctor ordered" for Spitak. Young, bright and also newly elected as Deputy of the National Assembly of Armenia (their Parliament), he has an innovative vision for the recovery and rebuilding of Spitak. Having graduated from the Economic Department of the Yerevan Institute of Public Economy, where he receives his qualification of economist in 1984, he possesses both the heart and desire, as well as the training, to help the town with their regrowth—literally from the ground up. The townspeople love and respect him and his progressive ideas. So do these people involved with Project AGAPE. He is a wonderful person with whom to work in meeting the needs of the school children.

Thankfully, thousands of other United Methodists in Western North Carolina also find it impossible to be indifferent to the great need for a school building, so funds immediately come forth to help with the project. Individuals from throughout the western half of the state send monetary donations, and additional money is designated from the conference to support the building of a new school. Bishop Charlene Kammerer of the Western North Carolina Conference is a key person in breathing life into this project.

There is a ceremony on September 29, 1998, for the groundbreaking and construction of the foundation for the new school. This naturally brings great excitement to the teachers and the students and their parents. "We are so grateful to people helping with this project in Spitak so that our children will have classes in normal conditions" is the statement heard time and time again.

The most important accomplishment for Project AGAPE during 1999 is the construction of the first subbuilding of Spitak's School #7 at a cost of $150,000.00. Volunteers from Western North Carolina go to help with the construction that will allow 150 of the students to have comfortable classrooms in which to continue their education. They still share stories of the impact of the devastation, and how difficult—yet inspiring—it is to see the countless tombstones all around them as they work on the facility, doing what their skills will allow. From the faces, and the broken-stemmed carnations, they feel a connection with each family, making their efforts all the more worthwhile.

A grand and glorious opening ceremony is held on October 13, 1999, with Armenian President Robert Kocharyan giving the dedication speech and cutting the ribbon. He both offers gratitude and commends the work of Project AGAPE in his speech. "I know about the organization of The United Methodist Church of North Carolina very well. They have carried out a lot of important projects since the wartime. They also work in the Kashatagh region. I have been in the hospital and in the Children's Home that were launched and are sponsored by this organization. They have contributed to the construction of Berdzor as well." As he concludes his speech, he adds, "I hope that the project will try to raise funds for the second subbuilding as well."

Mayor Suren Avetissian, Nara Melkonyan and several of the school's children join President Kocharyan in cutting the ribbon. The monumental ceremony is shown on the television channels throughout the country, and several around the world. A huge plaque hangs on the wall outside the school to announce that Project AGAPE is the provider of the funds for the school. Students immediately begin their education in their new facility.

Nara, recalling the devastating disaster, states, "I was a last year student at Yerevan State University during the year of the earthquake. It was awful. For several years people were unable to laugh or cry. Their senses would not operate at all."

Just as it appears forward strides are being made for Spitak with Mayor Avetissian at the helm, tragedy strikes again. As suddenly and as unexpectedly as the epicenter strikes Spitak, the mayor dies in a car crash on October 26, 1999, just days after the school dedication and opening. With the loss of his life, it appears his vision for the rebuilding of the town is also lost. But fortunately the people of Spitak have his vision embedded in their hearts. In addition, Project AGAPE is still a major source for help with medical supplies and education for the children.

(A further note of interest here is that on the day of Mayor Avetissian's fatal car crash, he was on his way to Yerevan for a National Assembly/Parliament session. He had called Nara the day before to see if he could meet her in the AGAPE office at 10:00 a.m., an hour before the Parliament session. She was to go to Berdzor that day, but agreed to wait until after their meeting to leave. After Mayor Avetissian did not show up at 10:00, she waited until 11:00, then 12:00. She tried to call several times but got no answer. It was only then she went on to Berdzor, and later learned of the fatal car crash from Rev. Jamie Armstrong, one of the AGAPE Board members in North Carolina, just as she hears it on the television.)

AGAPE carries on its work in Spitak when, in the year 2000, they furnish the new school with tables, chairs, blackboards and bookshelves, all funded by United Methodists of North Carolina. Several computers are also shipped to Project AGAPE for the new school. This project is completed in August of 2000, so it allows the students to begin a new academic year in September with their building now completely furnished. In addition, twelve new heaters—one for each grade—are sent to the school, along with the funds to pay for the electricity they will require over a four-and-a-half month period they will need to be in operation.

The school now has a large main center section, with hallways going off the sides—each hallway leading to one of the containers still in use to hold some of the grade levels. It is a source of pride for not only the students, but for everyone in Spitak. For students who have suffered the horrendous conditions for ten years to seek an education, the construction of a new building—furnished and heated—is almost unbelievable, and certainly extremely welcomed. But more important than the school is the gift of God's

AGAPE love they receive through the combined efforts of the project. And the greatest lesson learned by the students is that there is hope and a chance for new life.

Yet that is not enough for Project AGAPE. They see the need for a heating plant in Spitak to allow the schools sufficient warmth for the winter months. That becomes their project in 2001 with the progression of their help for School #7.

Unfortunately, economic conditions worsen and do not allow the construction of the next phase of the school. But Project AGAPE, through its construction of the new building, furnishings for the classrooms, and heat for the schools have helped the town to partially fulfill the dream of Mayor Avetissian who envisioned a restored and flourishing Spitak.

CHAPTER 12

The Beat Goes On

This book is full of interesting and unique characters, but none more fascinating than Dr. Artsakh. In fact, he could easily be called the "heart and soul" of the medical contributions of Project AGAPE, for he understands that even with his seasoned skill as a physician, it is the power of prayer that is the true source of healing power. He possesses an innate combination of skill and faith, and he passionately personifies both of those qualities, not only to his associates but also to the patients with whom he works. In an interview on the tenth anniversary video about the project, it is clear to the observer that Dr. Artsakh merely acts as the hands—God's healing hands in human form—

that bring healing to the people. It is clear to see that he also understands that.

"Dr. Artsakh" is not connected with Project AGAPE from its inception, for the AGAPE Hospital is not established until 1996, but he soon becomes a fixture. Because of his patriotism and dedication to his beloved motherland of Nagorno-Karabakh, which prompts his name change after the cease-fire agreement, he accepts the position of Head Doctor for the AGAPE Hospital once it is completed. Immediately he becomes "the heartbeat" of the project's medical efforts as his broad smile and distinguishing bushy fedayi moustache become a warm and welcome symbol for all who enter the doors of the hospital.

Before his arrival to Berdzor and the completion of the hospital, though, there are several important and relevant accomplishments, two in particular—besides the numerous shipments of medicines and medical supplies—that have a major impact on the inhabitants of Nagorno-Karabakh. The first one involves the purchase of oil to heat a hospital. From Charles Davis's December 1994 report, "AGAPE provided the only hospital in the Spitak Region with ten tons of diesel oil for heating in order to prevent it from closing. It is the only hospital within a one-hundred mile radius and serves an area that is totally isolated in the winter. If the hospital had not received the oil for heating, the hospital would have been forced to close for three-and-one-half months." One point that makes this effort even more outstanding is the extreme difficulty in getting fuel or oil in Armenia at the time. There are no gas stations and the only means for purchasing fuel is from huge tankers parked alongside the roads, more precisely rows of deep and muddy ruts.

In that same report, Charles also addresses the issue of starvation, which—along with severe malnutrition—creates a disastrous emergency. "AGAPE purchased 20 tons of wheat flour and 10 tons of vegetable oil from Iran to feed 18,000 refugees in northeastern Karabakh who were on the verge of starvation." This one gift saves the lives of those 18,000 refugees, an act of mercy for which AGAPE receives a commendation from the President of Nagorno-Karabakh.

Rev. Alec Alvord (Missions Secretary for the Western North Carolina Conference at that time), and orthopedic surgeon Dr. Angus Graham from Brevard, North Carolina, visit Project AGAPE in July of 1994 to evaluate further target areas and groups for medical attention. It is decided that four clinics are to be established and maintained by the project. One will serve Yervandashat and Bagaran, the two small villages situated on the Turkish border that can only be reached by access through a border guard post, which blocks the aid of other organizations. Since these two villages are only three miles apart, they are able to utilize a central clinic where there is already a building, a resident doctor, three resident nurses and a midwife. There is no running water, and the electricity is only available for a few hours each day, but still the clinic is functioning with ten beds, thanks to the initial equipment already in place by AGAPE.

A second clinic is situated in Tsapatagh, a small mountain village between Lake Sevan and the Azerbaijan border. Because of its distance from Yerevan and its inaccessibility during the winter months, this village is subject to many border clashes with Azeri troops. Due to its proximity to heavy conflict and the fact that it is frequently under rocket fire, there is very little humanitarian aid available for the village's 800 residents, who are all Armenian refugees from Baku. These villagers are preparing a building for use as the clinic, which, upon completion, will house four beds.

The third clinic is in the town of Kashatagh, formerly in Azerbaijan and where the heaviest fighting of the war occurs. With assistance from AGAPE, the people have set up a temporary clinic also with four beds. Staffed by a resident nurse, the clinic receives visits from doctors of Stepanakert three times a week with AGAPE providing fuel for the visits. A hospital that will house 20 beds is currently under construction in this village and is expected to be completed by the summer of 1995. (Because these villagers had to evacuate their burned homes so quickly during the past summer, they had no time to grab materials to winterize the shelters they find for "a home," nor an opportunity to plant or harvest gardens for food. They are the 18,000 whose lives are saved by the efforts of Project AGAPE.)

The last village to have a clinic is Aygek. This site, between Yerevan and Echmiadzin, is chosen for it exemplifies the unity and spirit necessary for Armenia to recover from its unexpected and downward spiraling course. The 1,100 villagers replant thousands of trees that were cut in order for them to survive the past two winters. They establish a community center and provide a building to be used as a clinic. A resident of the village serves as the nurse and staffs the clinic, which AGAPE sets up with four beds.

In addition to the four clinics, AGAPE chooses to support a hospital in Kapan, the southeastern corner of Armenia near the Iranian border. It is established "to care for the mass influx of soldiers and civilians wounded during the last months of fighting prior to the cease-fire." The hospital also cares for Azeri prisoners-of-war. Although there are 130 beds and the facility is staffed by excellent doctors and nurses, it is inadequate for there are no supplies or equipment.

It is during visits to these four clinics and the hospital in Kapan that the fortuitous meeting between Dr. Artsakh—who is then still Dr. Dalton Buniatyan—and Rev. Charles Davis happens. Dr. Buniatyan is a perfect match for the AGAPE Hospital when it later opens. "Dr. Artsakh," as he is legally, lovingly and respectfully called by this time, becomes an icon—"the heartbeat"—of not only the hospital, but the entire AGAPE project. He is not only a perfect match for the hospital; he is also a perfect match for the patients for whom he cares for they see him as a trusted friend and brother. The relationship doesn't end there either. It carries over to every missioner who travels to Armenia or who supports the efforts of Project AGAPE. A friend of Dr. Artsakh's, Garegin Mkhitaryan, says, "He was a doctor by profession, but had a great ability to penetrate into people's souls."

"The beat goes on" as Dr. Artsakh's role changes from saving lives of valiant volunteers to saving lives of ones who now live in a liberated, but disputed, section of his country. An extremely decorated war hero in one life, a very much appreciated doctor in another as "the miracle worker" commits to making the world as good as he can for the residents of his beloved homeland.

It is Tuesday, July 16, 1996, when the facility renovated by the local Berdzor government for the AGAPE Hospital is turned over to Project AGAPE. On Wednesday, July 17th, it opens its doors and the first eight patients are admitted and 231 outpatients are seen during the hospital's first two days. Although construction work still continues and water pipes are being installed, the hospital is in operation. There is minimal furniture, all of it remnants from the former clinic. The third hospital opened by Project AGAPE, this 20-bed facility is the only source of health care for the 35,000 people who live in the area, many of whom are resettled refugees from the earlier earthquake and the war. Dr. Artsakh, who has witnessed fighting and death on all the front lines, finds it difficult to believe that situations in Kashatagh are sometimes more heartbreaking to him than the war zones he's experienced, making him even more determined to do whatever possible for the people who are his own.

It is fortunate the hospital opens in the summer for it has no heat. Like the schools, the Children's Home and every other building in Nagorno-Karabakh, it is reconstructed from a totally destroyed building, a result of the war. Its 12-inch solid rock walls—the leftover foundation from which the hospital is built—allow for no steam pipes. Therefore, their heat source will need to be electric heating strips and a 20 KW generator that must come from the

United States. Yet there are no funds for either when temperatures in Berdzor approach single digits as winter arrives.

Although the temperature outside may be cold, the hospital patients sense the warmth of their caring doctor, Dr. Artsakh, and his caring staff. One of his most outstanding traits, among many, is the manner in which he strives to bring healing to the people. One of his patients is quoted as saying, "He has magic hands. Not to mention his heart." There are numerous tales of the lives he saved, both at war and in the hospital. Reports from surgeons of large hospitals tell of their amazement at "the lives of soldiers he saved having unspecialized instruments," a practice for which he is still known at the AGAPE Hospital.

One of the things that most perturbs Dr. Artsakh is the outrageous prices charged by doctors in the cities. He fondly recalls the days when physicians were paid with a hen or basket of garden vegetables and the people were more important than the money. Those are the days he also realizes that he sees worse situations in the AGAPE Hospital than he did in the battlefields.

Because of the primitive setting and the lack of medical supplies, all of Dr. Artsakh's surgical work has to be done with only local anesthesia. He is as elated as the patients several years later with the arrival of a general anesthesia machine that comes from "the benevolent souls in America." It will allow surgeries to be more comfortable for the hospital's patients.

Although the rooms and hallways of the AGAPE Hospital may look dismal and in need of more space, there is nothing dismal about the care and concern administered by the doctors and staff for the patients. The hospital, itself, brings an additional form of healing, for with each cry of a newborn baby comes hope for the future of Nagorno-Karabakh. It is important to understand that after the genocide there is a strong national feeling of obligation to repopulate with Armenian people. Decades later, after another huge loss of life—from the combination of the earthquake, war, starvation and lack of medicines to combat the insurmountable outbreaks of disease—the government again strongly encourages Armenians to repopulate. Now, however, as conditions are so slow to improve, many parents feel guilty that they cannot provide their offspring a better life. Dr. Artsakh, who had never delivered a baby before coming to the AGAPE Hospital and where he gets plenty of experience, loves the hope he hears in a newborn's cries.

In 1999 alone, the hospital serves thousands of patients and witnesses the birth of 110 babies. There are 600 pregnant women registered at the hospital. Sadly, because of the poor conditions for both the mother and child, some of the precious babies will not make it, as later stories will testify.

By 2000, there are 12 doctors, including Dr. Artsakh and 22 nurses on the hospital staff. The hospital serves the approximately 100 villages of the Kashatagh district through recently opened "medical rooms" (first aid stations) in a few of the villages. AGAPE provides funds to help the hospital purchase a means for transportation, which is vital due to the complicated geographic location and horrible roads that must be traveled to provide effective health care. Because AGAPE Hospital is the only free hospital in Armenia and Nagorno-Karabakh, people come from the Armenian towns of Goris, Abovyan, Shushi and other places for the free health care. This means that corridors are sometimes used to admit more patients.

The year 2006 arrives and, after ten years of service, no repairs have been made to the AGAPE Hospital since the day it opened. "Throughout the ten years," says Dr. Artsakh, "many people and different organizations came and left with a lot of promises . . ." His voice trails off, but only momentary, for within seconds his usual vigor returns with a deep appreciation as he speaks to a team from North Carolina who supports Project AGAPE. "You were the ones who didn't promise, but acted. You were consistent in your actions and today you are the witnesses of all the changes taking place in the lives of Christians, who several years ago had lost the hope for the future. Now you have been involved in those obvious changes through your Christian love and sharing. You are the ones who couldn't stay indifferent to the sufferings of your sisters and brothers in faith, following the call of the Holy Spirit, ringing in your heart and mind."

He ends his statement with a prayer. "Lead us into the heavenly kingdom and bring your mercy to those who need it." Those words sound the theme of Dr. Artsakh's dedication to AGAPE *and* the hospital.

There is an additional person who makes a promise that also materializes. An Armenian living in France sends a sizable check to the AGAPE hospital for badly needed renovations. Although it is not nearly enough to repair the entire facility, it is a great start, and brings about additional funds from other interested individuals and groups to help complete the renovation project long necessary. Other promise keepers are the medical personnel who leave their own practices to help the medically deprived in Nagorno-Karabakh.

One of those, who is no stranger to the medical world of Armenia and Nagorno-Karabakh is Dr. Steve Erlandson, who has made numerous trips to serve in the area. He is joined in 2008 by Dr. Ben Sanders for a two-week medical team mission. While there, they work with Drs. Gnel Madatyan and Karine Simonyan, and under the guidance of Dr. Shahe Baliozian, who follows as Head Doctor at the AGAPE Hospital after Dr. Artsakh battles an illness and is no longer at the hospital.

Like all visiting teams, medical or otherwise, Dr. Erlandson and Dr. Sanders are "treated with respect and openness by all parties. We were not denied access to any area. We were impressed by the compassion and motivation of all the health care providers that we met.

"Although the hospital is free, most patients cannot even afford to travel to the hospital," Dr. Erlandson reports. "Some of the remote villages are more than two hours away along rutted wet country roads." Their first day they visit five village clinics in the northern part of Nagorno-Karabakh, and the second day five clinics in the southern section. It is on this second day he writes, "After three hours on a rutted pot-holed bumpy road, we stopped at the home of the village's head man. After introductions, coffee and food, the health care sister brought in the ill and weak. We saw children with fevers and ear infections, weight loss, bad teeth, pneumonia, skin rashes and infections, Familial Periodic Fever, slow weight gain, malnutrition, diarrhea, infected bug bites, asthma, chronic cough, and orthopedic problems. We were greeted warmly in all of the homes where we visited. With adults we saw cancer, hypertension, diabetes, TB, bladder infections, osteoporosis, skin rashes, arthritis, CVA and gangrene of the toes. We saw bedridden patients near the end of life. We saw many persons with many needs."

One of the greatest contributions of medical teams is updated training for the hospital staff and screenings for patients. From Dr. Robert Bradley, who in 2011 serves with a team of ten medical team members (nine others serve as a construction team), he reports that doctors serve together, allowing them to "share each other's style of practice and knowledge by seeing patients together." This is demonstrated by Dr. Steve Kading, an American gastroenterologist, working alongside Dr. Gnel Madatyan, the Armenian gastroenterologist, "bonding well" as they learn and share knowledge and styles. "Another way we shared knowledge was through informal seminars with the medical staff, mainly the nurses. They were very interested in the discussion of emergency assessment and care offered by Rand, our Emergency Department nurse.

"Diabetes and hypertension were prevalent. Control of these conditions was not adequate for most of the people for a couple of reasons. One was the scarce supply of medicines and another was the lack of compliance by patients.

Interestingly, almost everyone checked his or her own blood pressure at home and took their medicine only when the pressure was up or they had a headache or were dizzy. They stopped the meds when they had no symptoms or when the pressure was normalized, thus creating a yo-yo effect with their pressure.

"On the pediatric side, I have two interesting observations. One is that the pediatrician did an intradermal test on each patient to whom she would administer an intramuscular injection such as an antibiotic. This was to be sure they would not be allergic. This would not be a routine practice back home."

Dr. Bradley ends his report by saying, "Geographical isolation and lack of finances for needed services such as lab, x-ray, medical equipment and medications are major challenges to the system."

One of the primary ways for all medical teams to help is to bring supplies or dollars to be used at the hospital and the clinics, similar to what Dr. Bradley's team brings and what is most requested by the Armenian medical staff—dressings, gloves, casting supplies, syringes and needles, blood pressure cuffs, stethoscopes and diabetes testing equipment and supplies. In addition, Dr. Bradley's team brings medical textbooks and a laptop computer loaded with the latest medical information.

Dr. Lusine Sargsyan of the clinic at Ishkhanadzor, near the Iranian border, states, "If they had given me diamonds, I wouldn't have been happier."

Medical teams, like building teams, are most welcome and appreciated by the AGAPE Hospital and village clinics, which strive to offer treatment to anywhere from 10,000 – 15,000 residents, depending on the number of refugees from the Azeri War who live here at any given time. The experiences prove to be an excellent training tool.

With clinics in approximately 20 villages, days are exceedingly long for team members who travel from village to village. Mornings begin with leaving the AGAPE compound at 7:00 a.m. and returning around midnight. It is a tiring adventure, but one more rewarding than words can express.

What is most amazing, at least to members of medical teams, is the "agape" love they receive in return for the work they are doing for Project AGAPE. "They are the true spirit of Christian hospitality," shares one member in awe. "It may be their last piece of bread but they desire to share it with us." The experience is beyond humbling for most anyone who has ever served on a medical team. What they soon discover, with little effort, is that it is the same humbling experience shown to **any** member of any team. It, like their faith, is a part of their culture. Another surprising quality of the Armenian people is the way in which they share the pain and also the joys of each other. Multiplying the food in sharing, and lessening the pain in sharing . . . is that not similar to what Christ's disciples did? *And to what Dr. Artsakh did,* one can easily imagine, as the beat goes on through a new generation of visiting doctors and medical professionals.

It is not unusual for a team to return to the States but their generosity to keep on giving and helping long after they are gone. For a medical team often brings supplies and/or funds for medicines and equipment that last long after they are back at home. Dentist Lusine Sargsyan is a prime example of that. She is the head doctor for the clinic in Ishkhanadzor. This particular medical clinic is also blessed with a dental room. When asked about her needs, she provides a list for the team, along with the instructions, "I will be grateful if even half of these items are supplied." When she is called to come to the AGAPE office to pick up the plastic bags of supplies, she is like a child at Christmas ready to tear into all the presents to see what has been left for her. For truly, what has been left in these stockings (plastic bags) is more rewarding than any toys that could possibly be found under a tree. Every single item on the list is in the assortment of bags, in addition to two first aid kits. "The beat goes on" through their contributions.

To understand the appreciation of everyone con-cerned, be it the medical personnel of the hospitals and clinics of Nagorno-Karabakh or the patients, one needs only read the following letter.

"I would like to pass the word of gratitude from the community of Ishkhanadzor, the medical staff of the clinic and the communities of the surrounding villages to Project AGAPE and the medical team members helping our clinic. You showed your good will and Christian love to the people that needed the help of doctors and the medicine you gave to them.

"May God bless you and your families, because we haven't seen many foreigners that will leave their comfort-able homes to come and help people in need. Now we can only dream that there will be more people like you who will visit us at least once a year to charge us with the positive energy that helps us continue in life. May God's blessings be upon you and your families. You are kind people!!! Lusine Sargsyan and everyone whom you have helped."

It doesn't matter the doctor or medical professional, which hospital or clinics are visited, what illnesses and diseases are encountered, it seems reasonable to say that Dr. Steve Erlandson captures the thoughts and impressions of all visiting personnel when he says, "We met some of the most gracious and hospitable persons that I have ever met. These were strong pilgrims living in a rough environment. We also sampled Tan (liquid yogurt) and Matsun (yogurt). We shook a pear tree to fetch fresh fruit. We consumed young goat barbeque. I think that we visited the Garden of Eden. It is definitely in need of more health care."

Dr. Karlen Balayan is now the head doctor of the AGAPE Hospital, which also houses space for a pediatric area and Dr. Danielyan, who is the pediatrician. People say children are the same everywhere, and that is indeed true, given the hand-drawn and colored pictures on the wall of the examination room for the youngsters. As in America, favorite cartoon characters are the subjects of their exceptional drawings.

The office of Dr. Balayan is simple, and the few books that lay on a shelf of his otherwise empty bookshelves are a handful of textbooks and older editions of *Physicians' Desk References*. Though the office and its contents are minimal, his expertise and care of the patients is not; nor is his hospitality. His secretary serves guests of visiting teams the rich strong coffee and opens a box of elegant chocolates, Grand Candy, which is indeed grand.

Many improvements and changes can be seen from that July day of 1996 when the AGAPE Hospital opened, but not nearly as many as the number of lives changed and saved through the gallant efforts of everyone involved with the hospital. From the doctors, nurses and staff, the medical missioners who come, and the monetary supporters of the medical work done throughout Armenia and Nagorno-Karabakh, everyone working together continues to "be the change"—a change that, like a heartbeat, keeps on ticking.

There is a most appropriate story shared by Rev. Jamie Armstrong about a young woman whom he meets during his March 2000 visit to Nagorno-Karabakh. It perfectly demonstrates how the gifts given through Project AGAPE continue to touch people's lives, as well as Dr. Artsakh's commitment to his patients and his people.

From Jamie's report, "Several years ago this young mother of two children lost her right arm in an accident. Shortly after this, her husband abandoned her. Rather than live in despair, she learned how to knit sweaters with her left arm only, in hopes that it would provide a meager income to support her family. Last year tragedy struck again. While working in her kitchen, the gas exploded, resulting in the loss of both legs.

"Dr. Artsakh operated on her at the hospital in Berdzor and continued to care for her. Sometime after she had left the hospital, he found out that a new prosthetics center had opened in Stepanakert, so he began to inquire about the possibility of fitting her for an arm and two legs. The issue would be cost.

"Last fall, Dr. Artsakh sold the Niva 4x4 that had been given to the hospital by Project AGAPE in 1997. He needed to buy a more rugged vehicle to cover the rough terrain in the region. The net effect of the sale and purchase was that he had some money left over. For a couple of months he asked Nara what he should do with the money. She replied that it had been a gift to the hospital, so he should use it as he saw fit in his work at the hospital.

"Now, with the idea of getting prosthetic devices for this young woman, Dr. Artsakh had a potential use for the money in mind. He took her to Stepanakert to be fitted for the devices. She received her 'new legs' on March 8, 2000. There are pictures dated March 11, just three days after the first time she walked again. One shot is of her coming out of the house for the first time on her new legs. As we watched her walk, Dr. Artsakh told us he had not seen her smile in the past year. 'Now she cannot stop!'" With that exclamation, the broad smile for which he is so well known covers the width of his face underneath that distinguishing long fedayi mustache.

Neither does the work of AGAPE Hospital stop when the remarkable Dr. Artsakh develops Parkinson's Disease. Even though he retires, he continues to work until 2008, when the illness will no longer allow him to work. It is a sad day for all who know him when this ex-fighter pilot and retired military man loses the only battle of his life, the battle to Parkinson's Disease on July 18, 2012. Yet the medical accomplishments begun under his leadership continue even today. They are still carried out by the dedicated and loving supporters of Project AGAPE who, over the past

20 years have shared their time, their talents their gifts and/or their service so that others may live. The beat now goes on through Dr. Balayan and Dr. Danielyan and the dedicated staff who serves with them, as well as through the support of missioners and contributors who continue to be the pulse of the hospital's work.

And for the mission workers and residents of Berdzor, it is a most pleasant and rewarding treat to hear "the beat go on" as Dr. Artsakh's love of life, and vibrancy for his motherland, live on through the laughter of his widow and grandchildren as they play, almost daily, on the AGAPE playground.

CHAPTER 13

All Creatures of Our God and King

There is something that stands out, almost from the time of arrival, when one enters Berdzor and meets the staff persons and specialists who are a part of Project AGAPE. They all have something quite unique in common. First, they are all extremely proficient in their work. But there is a trait that goes much deeper than that. They are all **called**. Called to a discipline of service in order to make life and conditions better for those around them and to offer the same light and hope, through their own work, that seem to radiate from Project AGAPE. Their caring attitudes and dispositions, not only about those they help but every living thing around them, seems as natural a part of the environment as the beauty of the mountainous terrain surrounding all of Kashatagh.

Although most all of the staff members of the AGAPE office in Berdzor, and many of the assistants who work in the hospitals, clinics or Children's Home, are from the Nagorno-Karabakh area, few of the professionals are natives, such as Dr. Artsakh, so desirous to live and work here to improve the situations for "his brothers and sisters." For those like Hakob Hakobyan (Principal/Director and English teacher at Berdzor's School #2), and Dr. Armen Elbakyan (the local veterinarian for the area and Project AGAPE)—both of whom are Armenian but not from Nagorno-Karabakh—they are here because they feel, or hear, a call to come to this part of their country to make a difference. Before speaking about the veterinarian, however, and the vital importance of his work with the animals, and those who tend them in the area of Kashatagh, it is important to first share a few words about the "creatures" themselves.

One cannot speak of a visit to the AGAPE complex without the mention of the AGAPE dogs from years past, with Bottle being the one currently holding down the complex. With a quick recollection of the four Armenian men who visit Suzanne Stafford with their humongous suitcases, clinking and sloshing, you'll understand the name "Bottle." Though the dogs may come and go (sometimes there is one and sometimes more), it is apparent that they, too, feel they have a role in the life of AGAPE. Like all of the dogs before him, Bottle is the first to greet all guests, and within seconds, knows whether the guest is a regular or a first-timer to Project AGAPE. He also makes himself "the keeper of AGAPE" the minute night falls.

An evening of Bottle's incessant barking means, in turn, a night of the jackals' howling from somewhere below, their shrill ascending pitches reverberating off the nearby hills and mountains like a chorus of stereophonic sound. There is one night when something is different about his barking, though. Rather than the occasional move from place to place, he paces back and forth across the elongated front stoop that runs the length of the Christian Education Center (CEC) where teams are housed, making sure he is never far from the front door.

The first member of the work team who exits the building for breakfast the next morning leaves the front door open, as is the usual habit. This time, however, Gayane—one of the AGAPE staff and the grandmother of two girls mentioned in a later chapter—comes running toward the stoop from where she is hanging out clothes. Although no one can understand a word she is saying, it is obvious there is a bit of terrorized anxiousness in her voice. Her hands go back and forth in parallel lines as her sounds become more frantic. The Americans, most of whom are now outside the building, stare at her curiously, some of them even mimicking her motions as they attempt to decipher her words. The scene resembles a lively game of charades until one of the team members yells, "Snakes!" Repeats of the word—some as questions, others as exclamations—come from various ones of the workers. It is obvious everyone now understands Gayane's warning.

"Ayo!" she exclaims in excited affirmation with their word meaning "yes."

Chatter from the rest of the staff soon indicates that a poisonous snake has been spotted near the front door. Bottle, whom the visitors now appreciate even more, is greatly rewarded during breakfast. He, and his innate perception of his duties here, are the topic of discussion for the remainder of the meal.

"Isn't it odd that this creature's presence here is as important as the jobs of all the rest of the staff?" asks one of the workers.

"And that he understands when he's needed and when he's not?" observes another, thinking of Bottle's perception of duty when the shipment arrived, by protecting it until workers took over, at which time he rests.

"Have you noticed that he sleeps outside Nara's office door when she is working late?" asks one of the women workers. "Or that he lies outside the door of her cottage when not barking at the jackals?" Her question brings an even keener appreciation for Bottle's understanding of his role and the enormous pride he takes in doing it well.

No one is surprised when the night watchman tells of a recent time he is on duty at the complex and a lone visitor is housed there, doing specialized work at AGAPE. "Nara had to go back to Yerevan to meet an incoming team. The entire time she is gone and the guest is here, Bottle slept on the front door mat of the building, his back curled up against the wood of the door."

Eyes turn to Bottle, who now lies content on the cool asphalt of the basketball court that is a part of the common area. No one has trained the dog. He has not been to obedience school. But he has certainly learned the ropes of caring for his charges. "And passes every task with flying colors," is the unanimous vote as breakfast is completed.

The point here is not Bottle; it is simply to demonstrate that whether a stray, a puppy from the litter of a dog already on the complex, or one given to the staff by a local, there is a perceived role of being called to service as the AGAPE dog. It is also a perfect illustration of how it is with humans who are called. As the famous saying goes, "God does not call the equipped; He equips the called."

As a beautiful black-and-white magpie—so common in Armenia—flies across the basketball court and perches on the limb of a tree on the playground, smiles don the faces of the work team. It is such a striking bird, whose sharp contrast of colors is symbolic of the sharp contrast between America and this disputed territory. The threat of jackals and poisonous snakes, and the appreciation of the magpie and Bottle, suddenly become a thing of the past as the workers set out to experience their next day of work at Project AGAPE, this time to visit one of the recipients of the Cattle Project, and check on his cow, another of God's creatures so important to this land and these people.

It just so happens that a veterinarian is with this particular team so he is greatly interested in the Cattle Project. As already mentioned in respect to other international organizations, Heifer Project International is unable to function in Nagorno-Karabakh due to political reasons. However, following their expertise and their model already in place, AGAPE is able to—with the help and support of the two North Carolina Annual Conferences of The United

Methodist Church—set up their own program called the Cattle Project, whereby a needy family is able to receive a heifer. A pregnant cow is given to a family, with the expectations that they are to pass on another pregnant cow within a 2 – 3 year period. If the first newborn calf is male, they have to wait until the birth of a next calf—which will be female—to be able to pass it on. That is why they are allowed a variance of time between 2 – 3 years, so that enough time is allowed for the cow to produce a female calf. This method of animal husbandry is a vital help to people in poverty areas for several reasons.

The family—or families, depending on how much money is received to purchase animals—selected to receive a cow are carefully and prayerfully chosen on the basis of how many family members there are and any extenuating circumstances that would create a greater need for one family over another. This arm of Project AGAPE's mission is far reaching for it allows the recipient family to have a way to produce milk, cheese, butter and sour cream – not only for the family but also as a means to sell their dairy products to the community, thereby generating some income. Project AGAPE purchases all of its dairy needs, both for the staff and the work teams, from heifer recipients.

The Cattle Project begins in 2006, and before the end of 2007, 43 families receive pregnant cows. There is no way to fully describe the excitement this new program stimulates and exudes from the families who are the first recipients, and continue to be recipients. For not only are they fortunate to become a participant in the Cattle Project, they also receive an incredible blessing with the promise of being able to pass on the gift to another family. To best put into words the vastness of the help this project creates, it is important to hear them from actual participants.

Raya Muradyan, one of the first 17 original beneficiaries of the Cattle Project, says, "My heart was filled up with an ineffable joy when I was granted this cow. This is a heavenly gift for our family. I'll be able not only to keep my family, but also to put a cross-stone on my husband's grave." There is a story about Raya's enthusiasm in the AGAPE newsletter after the first cows are given. She is quoted as predicting, "I'll be the first one to pass on the gift." Raya keeps that promise when in November 2008, she passes a pregnant heifer to the family of Susanna Tonapetyan. She proudly visits the AGAPE office with her two grandchildren to share the news. They are all greatly surprised when the two grandchildren receive the gift of two more cows, this time stuffed toy cows that have been kept in anticipation of the first family to pass on a cow. Raya is also surprised with the awarding certificate of "The Most Responsible Heifer Family" from AGAPE.

One of the key figures connected to Project AGAPE is Father Atanas Movsisyan (Director of the Christian Education Center and local priest for the Armenian Apostolic Church in Berdzor), who takes part in this memorable event by offering a blessing to both families and wishing them, and the project, great success in all future undertakings. His words, combined with his presence, offer great reassurance to Susanna who is in a horribly desperate situation with an eleven-year-old son who is all she has. She is overwhelmed and totally hopeless, unable to find any job or means to keep him . . . until she receives the cow. She writes, "I felt neglected, humiliated. My husband received an invitation as a specialist to come, resettle and take part in development of this community. I didn't want to come. He persuaded me and we came here in 1994. During all these years I felt sorry for coming here, as our dedicated work didn't receive proper repayment, justifying my intuitive reluctance. The only gift received here from God was our son, who was born in AGAPE Hospital twelve years after our marriage. And now when I am in a desperate condition Project AGAPE extends a helping hand to me. I don't know how to express my gratitude. May God bless all those good Christians far away who help people like me, reminding us one more time, that we are not alone. And thanks to Raya, who continues their kind work passing on the gift." Susanna's tears, now tears of hope and faith for the future of her family, fall freely as she offers her words of thanks.

One of the efforts with the Cattle Project is to get cows into the various villages of Kashatagh, away from Berdzor, so that families there can also be fed and hopefully gain even a very minimal bit of income by also supplying their neighbors with dairy products. The Mazmanyan family (Mher, Christineh and their six children) lives in Tandzut, in the northwest part of Kashatagh. Mher is an Azeri war veteran left with several wounds. A recent university graduate with a degree in economics when the war breaks out, he cannot stay indifferent to the sufferings of Armenia and Karabakh, and the danger knocking at the eastern and southwestern gates of his homeland. With no hesitation, Mher joins one of the groups of volunteers to protect the remnants of his country. The family now survives on the pension Mher receives as a handicapped person. His wife, an accountant, can find no work.

"I cannot sit without doing anything," he says in thankfulness when his family receives a cow. "I am so grateful for this great help to my family. The only way to show my gratitude is to take good care of the cow that will feed my children, grow my own farm and help a family like ours."

Another family to receive a cow lives in a village near the border of Iran. Karine Gogoryan's family moves there after their home in Giumry, the largest city in the north of Armenia, was—like the entire city—completely destroyed in the 1988 earthquake. Like many of the earthquake survivors who lost everything, they are given a small plot of land to come to Karabakh and resettle with the hope and promise of starting a new life. It is not until December 2009, when there is absolutely no other hope, that Karine approaches AGAPE and requests an audience with Nara.

"We lost the house, everything we had acquired during our whole life. We decided to come and live here as the soil here is good and the climate is better, compared with the inclement climate of the north, hoping that this could be a better place to start a new life and stand again on our own feet. We were granted a "shelter" – 22 meters square (approximately 26 yards square) with one acre croft. We live in that one small room with our seven children and my mother-in-law, ten people in one tiny room. My husband and I cannot find a job, as it's difficult to find any job in that small village. The only way to feed our family is to work on our croft, but we don't have tools and equipment to process the soil and no transportation to take the possible crop to the market. When I was coming here I saw a charwoman cleaning the street. I am an accountant, but I would wish to have a work like that to be able to somehow feed my seven children and not feel guilty for giving life to them. We lost many of our relatives in the earthquake. After the Azeri War and the earthquake, inspired by patriotic ideas, we had seven children. Now I feel sorry as I cannot provide even minimum conditions for them.

"This is the first time I apply to AGAPE with a request to help my family, as my pride didn't let me do that before. Now we are in a desperate condition close to starvation and the only place I knew would get understanding and empathy is AGAPE. It's humiliating to be in a role of a beggar, especially for my husband (it was shameful for him to come with me and he is waiting outside) and me, as we are able to work and we want to work. Just give us a 'small air,' help us to help ourselves and we'll be more than grateful to you. Please come and see the conditions we live in and you'll better understand me."

Tears stream down Karine's face as she opens her heart and soul to Nara. She is given financial help there on the spot, but Nara and the staff are aware it will only suffice for a short term for the Gogoryan family. There is a promise to visit, see the conditions firsthand and analyze the best ways to help the family. That promise, with other assistance along the way, brings a "small air" to allow the family to start breathing freely and be able to feed the seven children as they receive a pregnant cow from Project AGAPE in August of 2011.

The Cattle Project serves in another meaningful way. Two of the cows passed on from the original 17 families go to the Children's Home as a part of a micro-project. The cows—in addition to providing the children their own source of dairy products—also allow the children a knowledge and skill of new methods that will enable them to become good farmers and successful in their lives.

For the many families who are recipients of cows, 109 as of the writing of this book and knowledge of a couple of others by Christmas 2014, one of the greatest rewards of the Cattle Project is the gift of being able to reach out and help brothers and sisters through the passing on of a pregnant cow. Along with the Children's Home, another of those who receives a blessing in November 2009, with the passing on of heifers from the original 17 families, is Samvel Dallakyan.

Samvel, a father of eight and grandfather of one, lives in a village near Berdzor and, having received help in several ways, is well known to AGAPE. The Dallakyan family makes its living by caring for cows that belong to other farming families in the community, but the fee they receive in return is so small that it does not even buy bread for eleven people. "This is one of the blatant injustices of life: those who can afford cows don't have skills and cannot care for them while others who cannot afford buying a cow can do it perfectly," notes a staff person.

The youngest of Samvel's children, Lianna, is especially happy they have their own cow. "She goes to the barn and caresses the cow," says Samvel cheerfully. "AGAPE's assistance is and has always been invaluable for our big family. We worked hard for others. Now we'll take care of our own cow, and that's thanks to your help. We are happy that our children are excited and now will help us with double enthusiasm. My father always told me, 'Do for others, learn for yourself.' Now I understand the wisdom of our elderly.

"He also said, 'Man is not known for what he saved, he is praised for the charity he gave.' Now I pass the wisdom of my parents to my children hoping that they'll become good people and useful for the humanity like those who have helped us during these difficult years and continue to help. MAY THEY BE BLESSED AND PRAISED FOR THE CHARITY THEY GIVE."

These testimonies speak to the value not only of the humanitarian aid assistance, but especially of its Cattle Program. However, this substantial addition to the work of Project AGAPE and its continued success does not just happen. Dr. Armen Elbakyan, who felt the call to come to this area in 1999, is the veterinarian involved with Project AGAPE who checks each heifer received to be sure it is in good health. He also oversees the birth of the calf and ensures its safety and health, as well. A part of the money used to provide a cow for a family also includes any necessary veterinary services and medicines. Dr. Elbakyan's faithfulness to his work and to the people is a vital part of this program.

Much of the success of Project AGAPE's Cattle Project is the tenacity, self-respect and hard work of the Armenian people. They take care and pride with what they do have, no matter how little it is, using it to its fullest.

This is no different with those who are participants in this program. One of the most amazing success stories of the Cattle Project involves a man who is one of the first 17 recipients of cows. From the gift of that first cow, he is actually able to create a business for himself in animal husbandry. He now manages to breed enough offspring that several of the animals purchased for the Cattle Project come from his business.

Once a new cow is purchased, as necessary monies come in from individuals, churches or groups, Dr. Elbakyan also carefully examines it to make sure it is healthy and in fine condition to begin its placement with a new family. When the cow is presented to the family, Dr. Elbakyan then marks it with a numbered tag so that it, and any offspring, can be kept up with for further treatments or veterinary needs.

As with everything that Nara oversees in her capacity as the Country Director for Armenia, the efficiency of the Project AGAPE's staff is top notch. It is no different with the work of Dr. Elbakyan. There is another noteworthy quality about Dr. Elbakyan. He is charming, witty and makes you feel immediately welcome to the area and his office, located just outside Berdzor, which he has spent most of his own money renovating and reconstructing. Also a bombed shelter, one would never know it from the way it appears now. The view from his office competes with that of any resort anywhere in the world. From the spacious front porch he has built, one wonders whether he could ever become complacent with the magnificence of God's world all around him.

But then, within moments of meeting him, you perceive his love and dedication to not only the animal kingdom, but the residents of Kashatagh. There is a small building, more like a shed, at the front entrance of his office. This is where he sells medicines for animals that are not a part of the Cattle Project. Most of the medicines are given freely, however, as he understands the conditions of those with whom he works. Therefore, his work is his life. There is only one way to most adequately describe Dr. Armen Elbakyan, who is a noted source for many veterinary publications of Armenia. He is exactly like Dr. Doolittle . . . Armenian-style.

The good vet's work is not done alone. He has an incredible staff, one of whom—Lilia, who is a phenomenal baker and also the sister of Arthur, AGAPE's night watchman—is studying veterinary medicine and is a wonderful assistant. Already, with the success of the Cattle Project, there is such a need for veterinary services in Kashatagh that another vet, a female, serves the outlying villages a few days each week.

People aided by his expertise, both with the Cattle Project and their other animal needs, are most thankful to have him at their service. But, Margarit Mazoulyan, a resident of the village of Vaghazin in the northern portion of Kashatagh—also a Cattle Project recipient and the mother of twelve children—realizes that Dr. Elbakyan, God and Project AGAPE are not the only ones responsible for the help she receives. She understands there are many unseen contributors who make the work of the project possible. "I am so grateful to Project AGAPE for the continuous help my family has received. I wouldn't be able to raise my twelve children if not for the help of Project AGAPE. The clothing, the shoes, the school and hygiene products we receive from your organization on a regular basis are an invaluable help for our big family. And now, this great gift, the cow, is a big help for our big family. I don't know how to express my gratitude and appreciation for all you have done for us. May God bless all those people in that far away country who help my family and keep them in His loving hands."

God's children, in that faraway land of Armenia and points between, are each—like the cows and other livestock, the jackals, the snakes, the magpies and Bottle—one of God's beautiful creatures. The first words of a hymn by St. Francis of Assisi, written shortly before his death in 1225, best state the partnership and ongoing success of the work happening between Project AGAPE, the ones who support it, the ones who deliver the work, the ones served, and the creatures that are also a part of its existence: "All creatures of our God and King, lift up your voice and with us sing, Alleluia! Alleluia!"

CHAPTER 14

Well Built

He is like a man building a house, who dug deep, and laid the foundation upon rock; and when a flood arose, the stream broke against that house, and could not shake it, because it had been well built. Luke 6:48

"Christianity—as in the woven rugs for which Armenia is so well known—is the thread woven through centuries of Armenian culture that has kept the people together throughout all of history." This statement, made by Rev. Mark Barden, Former Director of Missions for the Western North Carolina Conference of The United Methodist Church, offers a mentally picturesque understanding of exactly how important Christianity and faith are to the Armenian people. No matter the adversity, the oppression, the natural disaster—the list goes on and on—Armenia stands firm, and has for 1700 years, on its Christian faith and beliefs.

There is a statement made by Australian Senator Douglas Darby during his introduction of the Armenian nation at the "Captive Nations Week Committee Conference," held even before the fall of the Soviet Union. "If Jesus Christ carried his cross to Golgotha, the Armenian nation keeps on carrying it till this day." And with that cross, they carry the love of Christ and the strength of God as they take each step. They refuse to succumb to the trials that could have easily broken the threads of their faith. That is, perhaps, because the Armenian Apostolic Church has not only been the protector and preserver of the Christian faith. The accompanying and underlying root, that has enabled the Armenians to survive any challenge or misfortune that threatened to tear it apart, is that their Christian faith has also been the sole source of the cultural enrichment that has molded the Armenian people into the most peaceful, compassionate, and beautiful souls found among the children of God.

One of those beautiful souls among the children of God is Father Atanas, who singularly has more influence on the spiritual life and well-being of the community than anyone else in Kashatagh. Probably not a single person who lives in Kashatagh is unfamiliar with this dear quiet and gentle man. He walks softly on the earth, his hands ever on the black beads that constantly roll between his fingers.

To some they are considered worry beads; to him they are prayer beads.

There are some individuals in the world who symbolize the embodiment of Christ in their words, their actions and their spirit. Love radiates through their every act. Such is the case with Father Atanas. It takes no more than a couple of minutes inside Father Atanas' house, which sits only a few steps back from the side road where it is located, to sense the depth of his Christian beliefs. The house, small but welcoming, is filled with books. Stacks and stacks of books, all of which appear to have been read several times, line each wall and cover every table. It is easy to discern that here is a man of habit. He reads . . . a lot. He prays . . . without ceasing. He cares for the souls of the children and youth with whom he works . . . continually. He loves the Lord, his God . . . always.

Most people, once they invite a guest into their home, politely offer, "Have a seat." Not so with Father Atanas. He leads you into a room off to the right of his small, unassuming house, and you stand facing the outside wall where he has designed an altar, of sorts. And there you stand as he prays, long and ardently, softly and poetically, as the beautiful Armenian language takes on a chanting quality. It is a mesmerizing experience, and one that leaves you in awe as you feel you have truly entered the presence of God.

When asked to speak of his work with Project AGAPE, Father Atanas humbly defers to the work of the project as a whole, minimizing his personal work as God's servant. Yet his wisdom and care for humankind has wrought wonders through the projects and accomplishments of the children and youth as a result of the classes and activities at the Christian Education Center. As AGAPE's largest project of 2000, and under the priest's leadership, "the role of the CEC in changing the dull life of children and young people in the region resettled with refugees is invaluable." In creating excitement for the children and youth through the varied activities offered, it gives the church an opportunity to attract more children, thus keeping them off the street and away from any undesirable impact on their education. With such a great influx of refugees from different areas, created by numerous varied causes, the potential of the CEC in assisting the church to deal and cope with the expansion of sects in the region is tremendous.

One of the most interesting descriptions of this unassuming individual is that he is Project AGAPE's "best friend." That is quite a compliment, given the number of people involved with the project and the incredible roles each of them plays in its success. He blesses each family who receives a cow as a part of the Cattle Project, he distributes all the Christmas Shoeboxes at the AGAPE center, he holds the Sunday services at the local church, he plans special programs and events for Christmas and other celebrations throughout the year, and he meets with each visiting mission team. His duties encompass an array of responsibilities. Yet when funds are low, or worse, there are none, the dedicated priest continues to work, sometimes going months without even so much as a penny of salary. He serves in the capacity to which he is called.

Mt. Ararat

YEREVAN CAPITAL OF ARMENIA

Mt. Ararat serves as a dramatic background against the sky for Yerevan at dusk (top).

Yerevan is home to buildings and dwellings of all types (above).

A tall television tower dominates the Yerevan skyline both day and night (right).

The Art Park is a popular place to purchase everything from art to antiques to household goods (below).

Notable landmarks in Yerevan include the new Cathedral of St. Gregory (above left), Statue of Mother Armenia (above) and the Cascade (left).

A young family marvels at the nightly dancing fountains show in Republic Square (below left).

The Genocide Memorial (below) features an eternal flame (inset) in memory of those who lost their lives.

HOLY ETCHMIADZIN

The main gate to Holy Etchmiadzin (above) serves as an imposing entrance to the headquarters of the Armenian Apostolic Church. The Pontifical Residence is home to the Catholicos, head of the Armenian Apostolic Church (bottom left). The peaceful serenity is periodically punctuated by the ringing of the bells (left below) from the oldest Armenian Church (ceiling of the main entrance - bottom right). Seminarians are frequently seen strolling the grounds (bottom center).

The Mother Cathedral of the Armenian Apostolic Church (above and right) is framed by the Main Gate to the Mother See with the images of St. Trdat and St. Gregory the Illuminator.

Inside the church is a museum (below) that contains numerous artifacts including the spear tip purported to have pierced Jesus' side (right inset) and a relic of Noah's Ark (left inset).

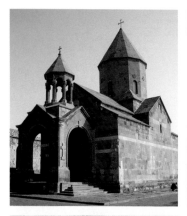

FAITH

The faith of the Armenian people enabled them t[o]
persevere through centuries of hardship.

The Church of St. Gregory in the Ararat Valley (to[p]
left), the pointed dome at Geghard (above),
Armenian cross stones called khachkars (left),
candles lighted in prayer (bottom left) and the altar a[t]
the church in Berdzor (below) are but a few of the
expressions of their deep faith and devotion.

Caves in the border village of Tegh (top left) were used as dwellings during the war years.

Abandoned industrial complexes from the Soviet-era (top right) are found throughout Armenia.

Beekeepers tend their hives during the summer throughout the Armenian countryside (above).

Storks build nests atop telephone poles (bottom left).

The grave of a single family in Spitak (below) is a reminder of the devastating earthquake of 1988.

Nestled on a hillside, Berdzor (bottom) is home to a new church (top right) built following the war.

A monument (center right) incorporates a clock stopped at the time the earthquake hit in 1988.

Roads in and out of Berdzor attest to the rugged terrain surrounding it (below).

The people of Berdzor have worked tirelessly to transform shells of burned-out buildings into schools, businesses, offices and homes (above and below).

The home of Project AGAPE (left photo - upper third) can be seen overlooking government buildings and the center of Berdzor.

A war memorial (bottom left) sits atop a small hill in the center of Berdzor.

AGAPE Center

The Project AGAPE Center features a Christian Education Center (above) where courses such as rug-making are taught (right).

Another building provides lodging (bottom left) and overlooks a playground (bottom right).

The staff house and warehouse (below) frame a courtyard with a basketball area.

AGAPE WAREHOUSE

Humanitarian aid is shipped in containers from N. C. (top left) and prepared for distribution in the AGAPE Warehouse (below).

Aid includes furniture (left center), Christmas boxes (above), food (left) and more.

AGAPE
CHILDREN'S HOME

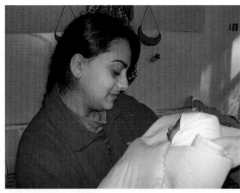

AGAPE
HOSPITAL

Dr. Artsakh Buniatyan, affectionately known as Dr. Artzakh (above) was instrumental in establishing the AGAPE Hospital in Berdzor (bottom).

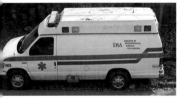

HOMES

Project AGAPE has helped turn burned-out shells into homes for the people in villages surrounding Berdzor.

STEPANAKERT

tepanakert, capital of Nagorno-
arabagh, lies in a valley surrounded
y high mountains (above).

prominent landmark is Grandmother
nd Grandfather Armenia (right).

SHUSHI

n old prison served as fortification
rotecting Shushi (bottom), which is
·cated on a mountain overlooking
tepanakert.

he first Armenian tank to enter
hushi is now a memorial beside the
ighway (below).

he church at Shushi (right) was used as
1 ammunition depot during the war.

PEOPLE

The determination and hope of the Armenian people show on their faces as they face the joys and challenges in daily living.

There is a famous quote by Homer, the Greek poet, in which he wrote of his friend, "He was a friend of man and lived in a house by the side of the road." Later, in 1897, Sam Walter Foss writes that famous quote into a poem this way, "Let me live in my house by the side of the road and be a friend to man." They could have easily been speaking of Father Atanas, who truly does live by the side of the road and is, without question, a friend to man.

Also by the side of the road, on the outskirts of the town of Berdzor, is one of the first building projects of the area - a church, simple, yet a strikingly beautiful structure. Not only is it a milestone for the area to have a church, but this is the first church built in Armenia in 250 years. Its walls of large gray stones, natural to the area, provide both a warm sensitivity yet a regal tone for worship. As with most every church still left standing in Armenia, it is an acoustical dream, for you can stand in any spot within the structure and lift your voice to the heavens and hear a perfectly toned sound. One of the work teams, when visiting the church, joins in singing **Praise God from Whom All Blessings Flow**. Though there are only a handful of persons, the sound could easily be mistaken for an entire choir of angels as their individual homogenous voices meet somewhere in the openness of the church and transform into a richly harmonious blend in the empty circular abyss of the structure, creating a heavenly euphoric sound that is beyond belief. The echoes, still circling the room long after the singing stops, prolong the worshipful mood making it difficult for one to move from the spot where he or she is standing.

To move from that spot and walk backwards toward the door—as is the Armenian Apostolic tradition of never turning your back on God—to look around and see signs of destruction still abounding, yet the "light on the hill" visible at the site of the Project AGAPE complex, there is no doubt that God's hand *and* voice are ever present in the work that goes on here. And this church, this beautiful structure where all the blessed inhabitants of the area can worship freely, is without a doubt "God's house." This church's foundation, as well as the spiritual foundation of those who enter its doors, is "well built."

In Stepanakert, once the capital of historic Artsakh and now the capital of Nagorno-Karabakh, stands the office of Archbishop Pargev. Pargev, who is appointed to this office just prior to the war, is here when the building is bombed at the beginning of the war. Because the Archbishop's office is considered the center of religion and faith for a country built on Christianity, it is also considered the town's strongest point. Therefore it is the first building to be bombed when the war begins. Not only does Archbishop Pargev bravely face that danger, he drives to the front lines of battle to pray with the volunteers and soldiers, and over the wounded and killed. His long face, lean and tanned, is a roadmap of his experiences, which are not only his personal ones but the ones of his flock. As he begins to speak of his call to ministry and the dangers he has faced, it takes no time to realize that you are in the presence of a miracle. As you visually survey the reconstructed beautiful edifice and surroundings of this holy complex, you perceive that it—like the man housed inside and the people he serves—is "well built."

As Echmiadzin is the Holy Center for the Armenian Apostolic Church, so is Shushi for Nagorno-Karabakh. There is a beautiful church there, holding an impressively demanding spot on the jagged white cliff, so unusual for the black mountains of the area. The church is the focal point of the entire area, bringing in hundreds of people for worship, weddings or any other service of the faith. An uplifting moment occurs when a large group of soldiers leave the Sabbath service and load a bus, filling it to capacity, to return to their base.

Children run and play on the expansive flat concrete pad built on the top of the white cliff that is the foundation for not only the sanctuary, but also the bell tower and the various gathering spots where worshippers can meditate at this place now considered "Holy Ground." An old woman, bent from age, enters the service with her candles, ready to light them and pray (pictured in the photo section). One look at her and her strength, even in her weakened state, symbolizes a life "well built" in the faith.

On the outskirts of Shushi is a tank, a monument to the war. What stands out and makes the tank unusual is the white cross painted on its side, creating an awareness that the Armenian men of that battle were not only fighting to reclaim their ancient territory, but also for the freedom to display that cross. This is the first tank that was able to push through this point, considered the stronghold of the war. It is important to understand that this country, on the heels of the collapsed Soviet Union, did not even have an organized army at the time. The white cross on the side announces the sentiment of the entire Armenian nation, for every Armenian—including spiritual leaders and seasoned military officers—will tell you that God won this battle where the higher ground was overtaken and rocks and stone overtook shells and guns. These are the same rocks and stones that are the foundation of all the buildings and structures in this area that is, again, proudly "well built."

To totally understand and appreciate the fullness of the term "well built" to Christianity in Armenia, it is important to understand a bit of the country's spiritual background. It is said that Thaddeus and Bartholomew, two of Jesus' disciples, first brought Christianity to the ancient land of Armenia during the first century. They are also rumored to have brought the Spear of Christ—the spear used to put into Jesus' side at his crucifixion—to the country and hidden it away in a cave. The spear (pictured in the photo section), along with relics of Thaddeus and Bartholomew, petrified pieces of wood from the ark and many other treasures of the country's religious history, is housed in one of the museums at the Mother See.

The Mother See of Holy Echmiadzin is the spiritual and administrative headquarters of the worldwide Armenian Church. Founded by the Descent of Christ and built by St. Gregory the Illuminator and King Trdat III in 301 AD, the Mother Cathedral has long stood as a symbol of the Armenian faith, nation and people and is recognized by Armenians around the world.

The Mother Cathedral is the oldest church built by a state in the world. It is on this spot that St. Gregory the

Illuminator has a vision of Christ descending from heaven and striking the earth with a golden hammer to show where the cathedral should be built. Hence, the patriarch gives the church and the city the new name of Echmiadzin, which is translated as "the place where the Only Begotten descended." St. Gregory, a religious leader at the time, is credited with converting Armenia from paganism to Christianity in 301 AD, making Armenia the first nation to adopt Christianity as it official religion.

Many who read this book will be familiar with the phrase "One, Holy, Universal and Apostolic Church" that is spoken in the Nicene Creed of many denominations. Throughout all of Christianity, these Four Marks—or attributes of the Church, depending on a particular denomination's terminology—remain and represent what historically have been considered the most important affirmations of the Christian faith.

Holy Echmiadzin is not only a place of worship and baptismal services, it is the residence of the Catholicos, it houses the seminary and dorms, it includes museums and a bookstore, and its beautifully landscaped flower gardens provide a quiet place to rest and meditate and join with others in the faith. There is one particular man, a 90-year-old veteran of WWII (pictured in the photo section) who comes and sits on one of the many benches along the sidewalks of the holy center each day. Dressed in the same fedora and old suit jacket daily, with all of his military badges and medals covering the entire front of the jacket, he sits and speaks to anyone who will stop for a moment as he shares his life's amazing stories, vibrant stories that speak of a person and a life "well built." His loving and gentle appearance, as well as his shining spirit—like that of Father Atanas—is another perfect example of how this background of religious history has helped to mold the Armenian people into the most peaceful, compassionate, and beautiful souls found among the children of God.

In addition to the religious foundations of Armenians and their spiritual lives, there is also another example of how "well built" the church foundations are; that is by the many church structures that dot their countryside. Throughout years of war, oppression and destruction, church buildings have been bombed on various occasions over many centuries. Even so, many of those churches have been rebuilt or reconstructed. One in particular is a 4th century church in Nagorno-Karabakh that has been bombed four times, and four times it has been reconstructed, each time using the strong foundation that has survived each particular bombing. There is a picture of that church that distinctively shows a different stone color or building line for each reconstruction. It is a visible example of the lives of the people. They may get knocked down by the events of the times, but each time the deep-seeded roots of their Christian faith allow them to survive and keep going, striving to make the best world possible for themselves.

Grounded in that same "well built" foundation, and with the help of many dedicated brothers and sisters of the two North Carolina conferences of The United Methodist Church—and other denominations and groups who are now joining them—Project AGAPE carries on this religious and cultural tradition through its many ways of serving the people of Nagorno-Karabakh. Still as the only organized humanitarian group working in the Kashatagh region of Nagorno-Karabagh Republic, Project AGAPE continues to refuse all funding that will endanger or prevent it from working in Kashatagh. It remains versatile so that it can quickly respond to any emergency needs that arise, but also seeks funds to implement development projects. The project's desire is that the people they serve may become independent and self-sustaining. So as Project AGAPE continues to adapt to meet the needs of this rural area of Karabagh where there is a heavy concentration of refugees and displaced persons, the major need for safe, secure and sanitary housing will continue to be one of the project's top priorities. And the project will continue to help restore the basic rights for the people of this region so they may live in conditions that are decent for human beings. It will continue to help Nagorno-Karabakh develop into a country where the lives and faith of the people, as well as their dwellings, are "well built."

(During the course of the completion of this book, Father Atanas retired following his last service in the Berdzor church on January 6, 2014, the day of the Armenian Christmas. He now lives in Yerevan with his daughter.)

CHAPTER 15

It Happened One Night

It has been an exciting couple of days in the Kashatagh region of Nagorno-Karabakh. Nara, Hakob, two of Hakob's nephews and the AGAPE administrative assistant have all just completed the February distribution for the town of Berdzor, as well as the outlying villages. The recent shipment of several containers allows them to help the many families with their needs. From their exuberant smiles and spirits that come from the sharing of the distribution, it is safe to say they are as enthusiastic about the opportunity to offer help as are the ones who receive the aid. Once again, the AGAPE Center proves to be "the city of light" for the residents of Kashatagh.

The next couple of days will be spent re-organizing the warehouse to prepare for the next shipments and to complete all the paperwork involved with each distribution. After that, they will return to the AGAPE office in Yerevan to take care of matters there.

They all retire for the evening to the AGAPE Christian Education Center on Saturday, February 12, 2000. Each of them comments on how grateful they are for a good night's sleep after the long hours of work that precede the day of the distribution, much less the actual event. This building, completed in the fall of 1997, offers much comfort and use for many. It serves as the administrative center for all the work done by Project AGAPE in Nagorno-Karabakh, and particularly Berdzor and all of Kashatagh. It houses all of the work teams. Classes in the arts and computer training are offered in its spacious downstairs meeting room. Sports classes are offered in the large open area just down the hillside in front of the building, in the space where a new playground is just constructed months before, in May of 1999. And, as now, it serves as the residence for the AGAPE staff and workers when in Berdzor for the distribution of aid and all of their other related work. In fact, the local administration is allowed to use it as an "unofficial gathering place" for celebrations and official functions, both for the administration and the community.

Nara is most grateful for such a nice place to sleep after such long days with the distribution. Although the preparation and work of each distribution is cumbersome and tiring, it is an exhilarating kind of exhaustion rewarded by the enthusiasm and sincere gratitude visible on all the faces Project AGAPE is able to help. It is a vision she wishes everyone who contributes monetary gifts or donates items to the project could witness. That is the last thought she remembers before she falls into a deep, restful sleep, during which she dreams it is raining. She feels the imaginary raindrops on her hair as she sleeps.

It is in this building when, in the wee hours of the next morning on a bitterly cold Sunday, Hakob awakes to the smell of smoke, or so he thinks. It is approximately 5:00 a.m. when he goes out onto the balcony (the rooms facing the front of the building open onto the balcony) to check, thinking someone in the neighborhood is either burning leaves or a woodstove. Seeing nothing and not smelling the smoke, he returns to bed. But shortly after he lies back down, he is certain he smells smoke again. He jumps up, this time opening his door to the corridor and realizes the smell of smoke is worse here. He opens the attic door, and when he does, the flow of oxygen inflames the fire more. Hakob barely escapes from the flashover (the most dangerous time of a fire when a room bursts into flames, triggered by a build-up of heat in a room), but manages to flee just in time to beat on everyone's door (there are only four upstairs bedrooms at that time).

"Wake up, wake up!" he cries. "Fire! Grab your things and get out of the building. Fire!"

Everyone inside hears his call of alarm and seizes what they can on the way out the front door. Local residents, within earshot of the commotion and sight of the "city of light" exuding a different kind of light, rush to help grab whatever possible from the first floor before the fire makes its way down to that level. A family from one of the villages is on their way to the AGAPE Hospital with a pregnant woman ready to give birth when they see the fire. They forget about the pregnant woman and the baby and rush to the AGAPE Center to help fight the fire.

Nara awakes only to realize her hair is covered in droplets of melted Styrofoam, not the imaginary rain of her dream. She is hesitant to leave, for she cannot reconcile herself to losing the building. Instead, still on the second floor, she rushes to the bathroom and grabs a bucket half full of water, there for use to flush the toilet, in a fatal attempt to put out the fire.

"It's useless, Nara!" Hakob yells in a consoling, but urgent voice. Full of pity, he says again, "We have to get out." That is when she finally runs down the stairs, stopping to rescue whatever is within reach on the first floor as she exits the building. Hakob follows behind her, grabbing pieces of furniture on the first floor as he goes. She stands outside looking back in horror and disbelief at the sight in front of her.

The staff and volunteers manage to retrieve most of the items on the first floor – the computers, the tables and chairs, and a few things from the kitchen. Everything else in the building is a total loss, all of the staff's personal effects and, what they regret more, the toys and equipment for the newly constructed playground.

Nara, gathering her senses once outside as the cold winter air brushes against her face, suddenly realizes that everything she has is upstairs in her room. She has an urge to rush upstairs to retrieve her most valuable belongings, but is at least cognizant enough to understand that would be sure death. She can still remember how severely distraught she felt as she stood there in the cold dark, watching the building burn. The drops of water she now feels trailing down her face are not imaginary. They are real tears.

Fighting the fire is impossible. First, typical of that time for the area, there is no water service to the AGAPE Center. Water still has to be carried in buckets to AGAPE. Second, Nara sends a runner to call the fire brigade. It is only then that they learn there is no fire brigade in Berdzor.

The fire, having broken out somewhere in the attic of the building, burns its way rapidly through the wooden structure of the second floor. Within five minutes, the roof structure begins to collapse. In only 15 minutes, fire takes out the entire second floor as it collapses to the ground floor. All that is left standing are the outside walls, 20" – 36" thick, of the first floor. It all happens so fast that it is more like a nightmare than a reality.

Nara calls her brother, Gevorg Melkonyan (Deputy Director of Project AGAPE and called "Gig"), to bring her some clothing. She has only the clothes on her back, which are her night pajamas. As she recalls this night later, she adds with a smile, "Thanks to God they were warm ones!"

All five of the persons in the building at the time of the fire lose all of their personal belongings. Nara loses her passport. But what troubles her most is the loss of her half-carat diamond earrings she has worn daily since the age of 15, the ones given to her by her parents on her 15th birthday. She also loses two gold rings and a silver ring, mostly gifts from her sister, Lusine. Lusine later orders the same rings again for Nara, and even offers the gift of her own diamond earrings, which she also received on her 15th birthday from their parents.

When one looks at his or her own loss, in comparison to all the individuals who have just been helped through the distribution, it does not lessen the sorrow and pain felt for the loss of belongings, especially ones that are treasures from special people and relatives. However, it does put things into perspective of having little and having much. Especially when the neighborhood children of Berdzor, who have so little—nothing save the donations they receive from Project AGAPE—search the ruins for Nara's earrings and rings. She is so touched by their effort that one day later, when they bring a huge melted piece of a golden-color metal, asking whether it is her things from the burnt building, she does not bother to tell them that what they hold is only a melted doorknob.

When the official report arrives from the fire investigation committee, the conclusion is that the fire is a result of faulty wiring. It turns out the cable used for the stove is actually a telegraph cable or something similar, giving the appearance of being very thick and well insulated from the outside. However, once the fire burns through the thick rubber insulation, the thin wire inside is swiftly "disrobed." Although it immediately gets extremely hot, the first floor walls are unaffected because they are stone. Consequently, the burning rubber of the "hot" wires travels up to the next level. This second floor—where the attic is at that time—also has a sheet of Styrofoam sandwiched between the wooden ceiling and the metal tin of the roof.

Therefore, that's why the burning wire trails up to the second floor and the fire starts in the attic, the space over Hakob's room. In fact, Hakob's room is over the kitchen area, close to the part of the attic where the fire starts. That's why he smells the smoke. They learn, all too late, that the electrical worker apparently did not use new materials, and he spliced many pieces of wire together. The combination of the intermixed copper and aluminum is a potentially deadly combination . . . and almost was.

This tragedy, as horrible as is, helps to shape the future character of the ministry of Project AGAPE, as well as the area. Changes happen not only for AGAPE, but also within the scope of the official administration for Kashatagh. A "new" and direct water line is immediately run to the AGAPE Center that will provide non-stop water service. A local volunteer fire brigade is also immediately organized and trained for emergencies.

As a result of the fire, other precautions are addressed. One of the best is fire inspections in many of the area buildings, both for their current electrical wiring and their fire preparedness. This includes the AGAPE Hospital clearing all of its hallways and exits in the event an emergency evacuation is ever necessary. In the words of Rev. Mark Barden, former WNCC Director of Missions, from Project AGAPE's Tenth Anniversary video, "The flames of the Spirit warmed the hearts of the United Methodists in North Carolina. Both Armenians and Americans alike worked hard to build a better building than the one that burned."

An architect is then hired to redraw plans for a new

building. One of the first things to be considered is whether the stone walls still standing from the outside of the first floor are in any condition to be used again as the foundation. Since they were bombed in the war, and now burned from the fire, the question arises as to whether it might be best to simply knock them down and start all over again.

Nara's father, Balabek Melkonyan, who was an architectural inspector during Soviet times, one day asks, "Nara, you do know that this is what I did for over 40 years. You've never shown me where you work or what you do. Why don't you allow me to go there and evaluate the situation for you, and we can determine whether to use the walls or tear them down?"

Thrilled that he has so generously made this offer, Nara jumps at his suggestion. Balabek travels to Berdzor with her to assess the situation and finds that the stone walls are still in fine condition; there is no damage to the walls from the fire. Even the paint on them is still brightly colored. The use of these same exterior walls means less expense than if the entire structure had to be rebuilt.

Balabek promises to oversee the completion of the rebuilding project. But, because the construction of a new second Christian Education Center is already in progress at the time of the fire, the decision is made to complete it before rebuilding the first center. To alleviate a possible chance of another situation of faulty materials, he stays and points out any inferior work.

Once this second building is dedicated, reconstruction begins immediately on the burned building, with Balabek continuing to oversee the work and alleviate any problems. Looking almost identical to the way it did then, with only a change in the roofline and the back of the building to allow for more space, the new structure—this time with all stone exterior walls, concrete ceilings and a concrete roof under the metal tin—stands proud and tall against the backdrop of the mountain. The experience holds fond memories for Nara of her father, and his willingness to oversee all the construction. As it turns out, the contractor tries to charge them too much—$5,000.00, to be exact—for the reconstruction. Thanks to Nara's dad, who verifies that AGAPE does not owe this amount, he saves the project unnecessary expenses as well as assuring their facilities are built to last.

In his mission of making sure no chances of anything similar to the fire ever happen at AGAPE again, Balabek winds up staying three years as a volunteer architectural advisor. But he is not the only one who watches the reconstruction with a careful eye. The head of the newly established fire department, also a product of the fire, watches the building's progress from time to time. When the project is complete and ready for inspections, he says, "This is the first time in this region that I have ever placed my signature on the fire department documents for a building without hesitation." He impressively adds, "This building is so solid and durable that if it was possible to raise it from the ground and move it to another location, nothing would happen to it."

Nara still keeps a photo of the burned cable in her office as a reminder that the horror that happened one night could have ended much worse. A situation that could have been deadly turns into something positive for Project AGAPE, thanks to God's protective hand. The situation, for anyone familiar with John Wesley's story of being "plucked from the fire," holds a vague similarity.

CHAPTER 16

From Here to There

Ah, the art of sending a shoebox to a needy child. It seems a sweet, simple task. Just pick up a plastic shoebox at church, if provided, or purchase one at the local store and then fill it with an assortment of items, which could include a toy, school supplies, certain toiletries, small articles of clothing, a piece of candy (that won't melt), whatever you wish. Sometimes a handwritten note or Christmas card accompanies the box, and one of the most important items is the prayer that sends it on its way. In some ways, that one shoebox seems such a menial task, yet it is an immensely rewarding gift for a child who would otherwise get nothing. For some children, a Christmas shoebox may include the first toy they ever receive. It is also a blessing for the one who prepares it, caused by the joy given in its preparation.

Yet it is no small task to send items, even as simple as Christmas shoeboxes, to Project AGAPE. They, unlike most collected shoeboxes for children at Christmas, do not arrive via plane or special trucks. Granted, shoeboxes prepared for other countries also receive the same amount of love and care prior to their arrival to any worldwide destination; they simply have an easier and much faster method of passage. In order to fully understand the amount of work and number of obstacles involved with sending a shoebox, or any other item that offers a better life to a resident of this disputed territory, you now have the opportunity to follow the path of a contribution.

Items for Project AGAPE are taken to the Mission Response Center (MRC) in Terrell, North Carolina, which is sponsored by the Western North Carolina Conference of The United Methodist Church. In addition to being a facility where UMCOR (United Methodist Committee on Relief) stores equipment when not deployed, the facility provides space for the sorting, repacking and shipping of material resources to various mission projects throughout the world. Thus, there is always an array of large metal shipping crates filled to some point of capacity and being prepared for the various needs of countries around the world, as well as those in our own country.

Fortunately, on the day chosen to get a birds-eye view of the process entailed to get items from the hands of contributors to the hands of the needy supplied by Project

AGAPE, a team of workers from a United Methodist congregation is at the facility. After a two-and-a-half hour ride, the group of adults is busily packing the boxes that will go on the next shipping container to Armenia. There is no doubt, from the way they work, that this "is not their first rodeo."

"This is our 52nd time bringing a group here," one of the men in the group shares anxiously.

The shock of 52 visits is one's initial reaction. But then the shock is replaced as the mind mentally begins to do the math. If you consider 52 trips here, at 5 hours per round trip, not even counting how many individuals are included in each visit or the number of hours worked per visit, it is an enormous contribution of manpower. And all of it given simply to make the world a better place for people who are in less fortunate conditions, not to mention they are nameless, faceless unknown persons. Agape (love) is no longer a noun. It is a verb and the scene at hand is agape in action. The comment, "God's hand at work," suddenly becomes an actuality instead of a group of words, except this vision is a perfect example of God's "hands" at work.

"Yep," the man states again, proudly but not boastfully, "52 times." He is bubbling with joy that he is fortunate enough to be a part of such a caring congregation. There is something refreshingly comforting and inspiring about seeing a man this giddy over helping others. His reaction is enough to bring sheer delight to the soul. "We come one day a month, starting in late January through April. We don't come in the hot summer months because it's too hot in here to do anything, but we start back again in September, and then we don't come in December."

Another man joins the conversation. "We brought 16 people today."

A natural response to that would be a congratulatory "That's great!" Before anyone has a chance to speak, however, the first man adds, "But as large as our church is, we should have twice that many people coming to help." His earlier cheerful tone is now one of remorse. "Not only are they missing the opportunity to do something for others, they're missing the fellowship."

Even a quick glance at the people assembled here proves it has been "a jolly ol' time" on their way here this morning. *And that it will be on the return home.* Their camaraderie is apparent as they work together, not missing a beat of their rhythm as they converse.

"I've been here 13 times," offers another man. "Most of us in the group have worked here several times together."

"It's my first time," adds one of the women, "but I'm already sure I'll be coming back."

There is an energy flowing between them as they carefully sort, count, label and pack each box before placing it in the large metal shipping crate. Accuracy is crucial with this part of the job, for there are strict regulations for customs which, after years of experience, have been perfected by both the shipper and the receiver. Therefore all items are specifically marked prior to shipment. Because this process has been so finely tuned, it now only takes Nara up to three days to claim and retrieve each shipment as it passes through customs once it reaches Armenia. That seems an extensive period of time, but compared to earlier days, when clearing customs was a nightmarish ordeal that sometimes took up to three months, the process is now a breeze.

"There were times the goods had to wait in a Yerevan warehouse for a month or more till getting to Berdzor and being delivered to the families in need," Nara has explained. "And there were times when I was in Berdzor when the shipment came to Yerevan. I would leave for Yerevan, manage to do the clearance in one day and take it back to Berdzor with me the next day. It mostly depended, and still depends, on the inventory in the shipment. There were times when we had to obtain security certificates through laboratory analysis for all health, hygiene, medical and food items, sometimes even the soft and hard toys. Getting medicine was a real nightmare. Every new name in the inventory list raised a question: should it get a security certificate? Now we get those only for the food items.

"One of the reasons for the increased ease in receiving shipments is due to our current cooperation with UAF (United Armenian Fund), which helps AGAPE in transporting the shipments and which has an agreement with the Armenian government that all the documents and duty free/tax exemption papers are to be processed by the time the shipment arrives in Yerevan. That has made a huge difference."

Nara's professionalism and expertise, as well as that of volunteers at MRC have now made this a painless process. Although it makes for more precise work on the shipping end, it lessens the time required for claiming the items, so the overall time is shortened tremendously.

So, on this particular day, the labor of love to make shipping as painless as possible is in action. Women count, sort and inventory each garment by whether it is new or gently used, for men or women, and by sizes for children. Men count and box blankets and hoist furniture—including cribs, sofas, wooden and swivel chairs—to an area where they will be packed directly onto the massive shipping container used for trucking the items to and from ports.

It is especially interesting to note that a church of another denomination has sent scores of t-shirts and hoodies for the school children and the children of the orphanage at Project AGAPE. Of little wonder, also, is the fact that the t-shirts are NC State red and the hoodies are Carolina blue. This particular church has also sent tables and chairs for the school and orphanage, as well as blankets for many families to help endure the intensely cold winters, shoes for women and children, clothes—including coats—for women and children, and an array of toiletries. It is quickly noted that these are items specifically suggested by Nara as necessities for families helped by the project.

At first, it seems odd that fewer items are sent for men, but then it only takes a moment to determine the demographics of the area to be supplied by this shipment, thereby clarifying the reason behind that. Many of the men who would have inhabited Nagorno-Karabakh died in the war effort. There are many more women and children than men, so the need for them is less—at least in regards to clothing and shoes. The men's need is for tools and building supplies, for livestock and simple farm equipment, which typically comes through monetary gifts sent to Project AGAPE. Many of the work teams who travel to Armenia supply these items, either by leaving tools they take for working, or by contributions from their supporting congregations.

After this group completes their day's work, there will be still other teams who make sure that everything for the upcoming shipment is ready to go, which includes another segment of several-hour jobs by church volunteers who meet to palletize any loose boxes. For the Christmas shoeboxes, there are locations of churches throughout the two conferences that collect each congregation's contributions and then have volunteers to box, palletize and/or wrap the shoeboxes. Finally, after many hours of work by many individuals, the huge shipping container is now ready to be loaded to the hilt and picked up by a carrier truck. It will soon begin the long passage overseas, which takes approximately 45 days for the container to arrive in the Black Sea port of Poti in Georgia.

When it actually ships, Nara will receive a file of 3 – 7 pages of the itemized contents, which will grow to 15 – 35 pages by the time she goes to get customs clearance on the shipment. Prior to the shipment's arrival, she immediately begins work for the process by applying to the Committee on Humanitarian Assistance Coordination of the Republic of Armenia government, and then submitting all the documents of the file to assure the duty free or tax exemption allowance for all of the shipment's contents.

Once it arrives in Poti, a carrier truck picks up the container and begins the two-day trip to the terminal for the customs clearance office in Yerevan, where Nara meets it and begins the procedure to confirm each item on the forms. Once that is complete, the driver from Georgia either agrees to carry the container on to Berdzor, or another truck is rented and another driver hired to take the shipment to its final destination, where it reaches the hands of the needy.

Little does one anticipate or consider that in sending contributions—whether a simple Christmas shoebox or shoes, clothing or other necessary items—it is truly a labor of love . . . agape love.

Nara is making final preparations for a work team to arrive from Western North Carolina when she receives notification that a shipping container from the same conference has just arrived in the customs clearance office in Yerevan. Ecstatic, she hangs up the phone, praying that the container will reach Nagorno-Karabakh while the team is there to witness the awe-inspiring process of unloading the shipment. That is always the game plan, so that work teams can help unload the truck, but more importantly, experience the joy that comes with each shipment and understand exactly how significant their donations are.

She hurriedly makes the 30-minute trip to the customs office to verify that every box and item on the list— which for this shipment is 18 pages—is accounted for and in good condition. Excited that the container is here, she prays yet again for the improbable to become a reality so the team can experience the thrill of everyone connected with Project AGAPE at the sight of the badly needed contributions. A couple of days and no glitches later, Nara receives customs clearance and signs for the acceptance of the shipment. Sometimes the Georgian driver, who drives the shipment from Poti, will agree to take it on to Berdzor if he is not on a tight schedule. This makes the last leg of a container's journey a done deal. In this case, however, the Georgian driver does not agree. Thus the container is moved from the original truck, with the help of a crane, to another truck owned by a local transportation company called APAVEN (which interestingly means "Trust").

The work team arrives on schedule. After taking a couple of days in Yerevan to learn a bit about the culture, history and customs of the people of Armenia, and allow their bodies to adjust to the new time zone, they are anxious to get to work on the mission they've come here to accomplish. They set out for Berdzor, the capital of the Kashatagh province of the Republic of Nagorno-Karabakh. Their mission: whatever the greatest need is when they get there.

Volunteers, luggage, food and whatever can possibly be needed for the next eight days is piled into the two donated covered-bed trucks (a 1996 Dodge Ram 1500 4x4 and a Ford 150 XLT 4-door) that are as much a part of Project AGAPE as the staff and volunteers. The two drivers, Hakob Gumbalyan and Gig Melkonyan, work together like a finely-oiled machine. The eight-hour journey, most of which is two lane traffic and whose length is dependent on the weather and number of trucks around which the Ford and Dodge have to maneuver, always allows a welcome break for lunch. There is nothing boring about the ride through terrain ranging in appearance from the hills of Judea to the red rock mountains of the desert southwest of America to a western scene that leaves one expecting John Wayne to come riding from behind a rock formation of the Rockies at any turn. From stork nests atop tall posts near a hatchery, to countless "fresh air" markets in the backs of trunks or on a makeshift board (if they are that fortunate), to numerous beekeepers atop the mountains, set up like gypsies alongside the road for the good months (when the road is passable), there is no end to the array of Armenian scenery, customs and culture along the way.

Following lunch—which Nara always makes sure is in one of the few places available with delicious food, good facilities and a soothing stream running through the outdoor restaurant—one of the team members takes advantage of the opportunity to capture some of the gorgeous surrounding landscapes of the reddish-colored mountains of this area, with their jagged edges giving each summit a unique appearance. It is then he spots a carrier truck loaded with a shipping container slowly nearing the restaurant. He watches carefully as it approaches, making its way through the winding curves, and manages to snap a couple of shots of it with his camera.

As Nara and the rest of the group reach him, ready to "head 'em up, move 'em out," he shares the photos. Her eyes, as well as those of the rest of the group, light up with the expectation that this might possibly be the truck bearing items for Project AGAPE. There is one thing for certain. "It is at least the right carrier," states Nara.

The group hurriedly gets in the vehicles and Gig and Hakob set out in pursuit of the truck. Due to the surrounding scenery and the chase element of this scenario, the long trip instantly takes on the attributes of a western movie, with one exception. There are no bad guys chasing a train or stagecoach filled with a payload. There are however, good guys (and gals) chasing down a possible payload, only in this case, the payload is what will soon be distributed to hundreds of needy families. The Wild West chase is suddenly transformed into more of a Robin Hood adventure.

Because of its heavy load and difficulty in maneuvering the mountainous curves, the truck has not gotten far down the road before the group catches up with it. Nara checks her records for the container's identifying number and verifies that this is indeed the container bearing the shipment from Western North Carolina. The entire group breaks into loud cheers as the news is spread between the drivers. Both Gig and Hakob pass the truck, their horns blaring loudly as they waved excitedly to the driver. There is no description for the elation passing back and forth through the two vehicles. Anticipation for the work to be done accelerates.

Fortunately, there is a church not too far down the road from where the group has passed the truck. Newly built in 2001 to celebrate Armenia's 1700th anniversary of Christianity, it is a usual point of interest for mission teams plus it has sufficient roadside parking, making it a perfect place to flag down the approaching vehicle. While Gig and Hakob wait outside for the carrier truck, team members go inside the church to view the new structure, as well as to pray and light candles, as is the Armenian tradition. The lighting of the candles symbolizes the presence of God and Christ's saying, "I am the Light of the world." There is no doubt their prayers are a thanksgiving for the many items inside the truck that will soon, through "the Light," light up the world for many of the people of Berdzor and the border villages of Kashatagh.

Excitement fills the air when the team exits the church to find the driver of the truck engaged in conversation with Gig and Hakob. He seems as thrilled about their chance meeting on the road as the others. It is an overwhelming, yet humbling, moment . . . no doubt, God's hand at work. Chatter abounds between the team members as the chances are weighed that this shipping container—filled with donations from all over North Carolina—has traveled here from their home state, having left weeks before, and yet arrives here, on the same road to its final destination, at the same time as they have. Awe and reverence shroud the entire group, Armenians and Americans alike, as Nara exclaims, "God's hand at work!"

Of course, everyone understands this is not a "chance meeting" any more than the team member "just so happened" to spot the truck while taking pictures. The expressions on their faces allude to that. Suddenly energy and enthusiasm soar with the expectations of things to come during their visit to Project AGAPE.

CHAPTER 17

God's Hand at Work

Waves of energy, sparked with nearly uncontrollable exuberance, fill the air as the work team members arise the next morning. Though the night before brings little sleep (largely due to Bottle barking most of the night and the unfamiliar—and a bit unsettling—sound of jackals howling in the distance), their lack of rest is totally undetectable on the faces of the workers from North Carolina. For the truck, which finally arrived in the wee hours of the morning, is backed into position and waiting for its cargo to be unloaded in the distribution warehouse. That fact, in itself, is a miraculous feat, for Project AGAPE has only one entrance and that is straight uphill on a long unpaved road, full of ruts and bumps with washed-out gullies on either side. Not only do drivers have that to contend with, but there is a sharp y-turn that leads from the main street, which itself is so narrow that meeting vehicles have to go off the road's shoulder to pass each other. But then, when one considers the route and obstacles the items packed inside the truck have already endured to get here, one quickly realizes there is no stopping them now from reaching their destination.

Breakfast—although delicious and plentiful, and much needed for the tasks of the day—takes a backseat to the anticipation of helping to unload materials from one's own homeland. The workers chat, but the conversation centers mostly around the feeling of being caught up in a miraculous adventure.

Nara, as excited as the workers, greets everyone with her always-present vibrant smile and gleeful voice. "It is amazing that the truck arrived the same day as you. I cannot believe it!" But she, just like the visitors, actually does believe it, for it is a visible sign of God's hand at work. It is a sign that is already noticeably quite common here.

One point that becomes readily clear is those charged with the task of making things happen at Project AGAPE are quick to put self behind the work to be done. Hakob and Gig, along with Arthur and Sarmen, the night watchmen, are already prepared for the gargantuan task of unloading the truck. Gargantuan because, unlike in America where the driver simply uses a lift gate and pallet jack (or even better, a loading dock with a forklift and driver) to move the various items and pallets to where they need to be, what one sees here—willing hands—is what one gets. What takes a matter of minutes in the States involves several long hours here.

(Nara has been able to secure the help of four additional men from the area to help with the day's work. They are paid 2,000 drams each, which is equivalent to just under $5.00 each. This is average here, and it allows the residents to have work and earn money for their families, another positive influence of Project AGAPE as they try to help families become self-sufficient.)

The back of the truck is opened to reveal what everyone suspects – it is fully loaded from top to bottom with not an inch to spare. Furniture is piled high at this end, having served as a barricade for the other items so as not to shift during movement and now ready to be easily unloaded. It is impossible to imagine the joy these upholstered chairs, sofas and recliners, wooden tables and chairs and cribs will bring to the local residents for the joy stirring among the AGAPE staff and North Carolinians—working together as one—can be surely be heard from the mountaintops. These workers are like merry children at Christmas, only instead of stopping to examine the gifts, they are moving the gifts as quickly as possible to unload the truck and put all the donations in designated spots inside the warehouse. And to get to the other end of the truck that is filled with gifts of what essentially *will* be Christmas for the children here . . . stacks upon stacks of Christmas shoeboxes.

Once all the larger items are out of the way, the men from North Carolina and the AGAPE staff climb to the top of the distribution center, which is in bad need of a new roof. Monies from the church of the workers have been sent to cover any necessary expenses to make sure this new roof lasts a long while. It is fascinating to note that while the inside floor of the warehouse-type building is being covered—or stocked—with loads of "toys for all the boys and girls," not to mention the clothing, shoes and other household needs for the entire families, the building itself is actually being covered.

Left to unload the remainder of the truck are four men, who make up a team of "human reindeer," and a small rope. This team pulls each "sleigh"—which in this case are pallets, skids and oversized boxes—to the back door of the truck where it is then manually unloaded, box by box by the women of the work team. In this scenario, "Rudolph" is a thirty-year-old whose surname is Marzpet and whose given name is appropriately Governor (since he is the leader of the group, both in giving out orders and being at the head of the reins). One of the jokes commonly and fondly shared at AGAPE is that "the 'Governor' came to unload the shipment." His team consists of three older teens—Vitali, Zhirair and Arkadi—all 17 years of age and recent graduates of high school. While Zhirair and Arkadi are already attending university classes while awaiting their 18th birthdays, Vitali (Vito) will be leaving for the Armenian Army in a couple of days on his 18th birthday. Nara explains that a two-year military term is a requirement for the males in this country, beginning the day they turn 18.

The length of thin rope is wrapped behind Marzpet's neck and then under his arms, done the same way by the others behind him as they work in unison to pull each heavily-laden pallet. Because they were behind the furniture, the pallets are a good distance back in the truck. Once each helper gets some traction, the skid begins to inch forward, slowly at first until the men get a pace going, and then it moves steadily and evenly to the back of the truck where the women from North Carolina work in an assembly line to quickly unpack each stack and place the items in the distribution center.

Nara moves between the truck and the center, pointing the way for each box of contributions. The distribution center is amazingly well organized, with shoes and clothing all in one area, toiletries in another, household items and furniture in yet another section. Whatever comes off the truck gets taken to a specific spot where it will later be more purposefully organized to best fit the particular needs of the families in the Kashatagh province.

The team unloading the truck works diligently, taking no breaks, as their emotions range from laughter-laden joy at the sight of what has come from their corner of the world to a tearful humbleness of actually being here to witness and be a part of this end of the project. Strength mounts, as everyone seems to gain gusto rather than grow weary with the hard work.

Without warning, one of the women yells, "Listen!"

A momentary hush falls over the group of Americans as the Armenians continue to work, not understanding the command. Except for the sound of one of the skids scrubbing against the floor as it makes its way from the depths of the shipping container to the back of the truck,

there is silence. Not even the rustling of leaves from surrounding trees or sounds of children from the orphanage
up the mountain or the small farmhouse directly behind
Project AGAPE can be heard.

"What?" asks another of the team members, this
question being repeated by others who are also listening
but hear nothing.

"Bottle is not barking," answers the one who had
given the order.

Heads began to turn and notice Bottle, lying on an
old extremely-worn towel outside his lean-to doghouse
under the shade of a small tree. The Americans, one by
one, begin to comment on the silence of Bottle now that
everyone is awake and moving. He has barked to keep everything away from the truck during the night and now,
content that the work is safely in the hands of others, he
lies completely relaxed and oblivious to everything and
everyone.

With smiles of both recognition and appreciation
for the role played even by this seemingly lowly animal,
what others might term a "mutt" or a "mongrel," the workers quietly go back to their jobs of carrying boxes to their
appropriate spots. A valuable lesson has been learned about
Project AGAPE. Everyone—or in this case, every living
thing—plays a part in keeping the wheels of this invaluable mission turning. Nothing, or no one thing, is wasted—
including all the carefully-packed items inside the many
boxes being unloaded.

Though high spirits have accompanied each piece
of furniture or box unloaded from the truck, there seems

to be a level of heightened delight as contents loaded on the skids in the very back of the shipping container come into view. These skids are all filled with stacks of shoeboxes, most of them the clear plastic type with colored lids, although a few are actually wrapped cardboard shoeboxes. The first skid of the group is maneuvered by the four men to the edge of the truck, where stacks—depending on how many each work team member can hold—are handed down, six or seven boxes at a time. An assembly line is formed as each team member carries his or her armload of shoeboxes and replaces them in large boxes. There are even a few oversized metal shipping crates, open on one end so that someone can step inside to load and unload them, left from past shipments when the crates were also left for the facility. These crates are reserved solely for these shoeboxes and are quickly filled.

As the seven skids of shoeboxes containing hundreds of shoeboxes are unloaded from the truck, one point becomes quickly obvious. Children are the same all the world over. The contents of each of the shoeboxes, although somewhat different in content, are basically the same as what a child in America might receive. A quick observation while carrying these small containers, that will soon bring twinkles to the eyes of children in the area, allows one to imagine the excitement created by the items inside.

"Would the children rather have the clear plastic shoeboxes or the wrapped box?" asks one of the female workers, thinking of how gifts for children are beautifully wrapped in her own country.

"The clear plastic ones," Nara is quick to answer,

"for the families need those boxes to store things. They are used over and over, not only by the child, but also by the whole family."

Her words bring an added dimension to the task of filling a shoebox for a child. This mere plastic box suddenly becomes a more remarkable tool of ministry, not simply the act of a needy child receiving a toy and a couple of fun items, as well as a few necessary toiletries and perhaps a few pieces of candy. Each box, along with its contents, has a much farther reaching element to it, one that is possibly not even considered by the hands that prepare it. Unexpectedly, and without words, the complexity of this one plastic container is comprehended and a new appreciation for the annual collection of them is gleaned.

As the last stack of shoeboxes is carried into the facility, another sudden realization sweeps the air, offering all the Carolinians a moment of unified quiet reflection. Not only are they blessed by the opportunity of being here, to collect and arrange boxes of donations from their own homeland for distribution; they perceive how truly rewarding and astonishing their work here is, not only for both them and the people of Berdzor and the outlying areas, but how incredibly unique it is. The earlier excitement of the long morning is now transformed into a mystical feeling of awe at being a part of the only organization to offer humanitarian aid inside the borders of Nagorno-Karabakh. Instantaneously the impact of the totality of the work here is fully comprehended.

That is, until the last box is off the truck and the shipping container is completely empty. Sudden cheers, happy tears and applause fill the air, not at the work that has been accomplished, but at the overwhelming awareness of the many lives that will be touched through the combined efforts of the morning . . . efforts that began long before either this shipment or this work team left America.

"And the many lives that have already been touched through the gifts to Project AGAPE," voices one of the work team.

Without missing a beat, Nara offers the perfect coda to the day's efforts. "God's hand at work!" she exclaims, putting into words exactly what everyone else is thinking.

PART FOUR

A Life Well Lived

Looking Back

CHAPTER 18

Christmas in Berdzor

For Christians in America, it is difficult to put one's self in a position of not being able to worship freely. Although there are no "direct restrictions" for Christian Armenians during Soviet times, perhaps this explanation will offer a clear understanding of the way they observe religious holidays and events under communist reign.

Most of the population participates in the celebration of Christmas within their own families. This is observed on January 6th. They also observe Baptism Day, when everyone splashes water on each other to celebrate their baptism. Sunday morning and afternoon worship services still take place at the churches. The difference is that families of communist leaders fear openly taking part in these services and celebrations, for the communist party leader could lose his or her prominent position within the party or in the government. Although the communist party has an indirect means of keeping people away from Christianity (including the forbiddance of public sermons and Biblical training), there is no ban on church attendance. People are still able to enter a sanctuary to light a candle and pray. Nara tells of her own experience of going into the church before exams (this is still during communist times), lighting a candle and praying to be successful.

With that in mind, it is easy to understand exactly how meaningful and fulfilling the following remembrance of Christmas in Berdzor is. As Charles Davis says, "One of my highlights about being over in Armenia was my first Christmas in Berdzor. Have I told you about that? Remember, in Berdzor, we had that Children's Home. We had about 85 or 90 children that would come at that time. It is the same structure in the same location as now. We had a lot of children that would come in and we'd put them up on the sofas so they could attend school because they didn't have schools in the villages then.

"Someone once asked me if they had Christmas. I answered that I thought they had some kind of celebration in the early spring. You see, Communists wouldn't let them openly have Christmas, or anything to do with Christ. But they could have some sort of celebration on New Year's, and this jolly old fellow would come out and bring them presents. 'Winter Grandfather,' I think they called him.

"So I decided we were going to have Christmas there on December 25th, instead of on the day of Old Christmas, January 6th. I remember this well because one time I came home for Christmas and went back and celebrated it over there too. Anyway, I decided we were going to have Christmas in Berdzor. I had about a hundred people on a newsletter list, so in the newsletter, I explained that I wanted to have Christmas. I told them how many boys there were, and how many girls, and then counted all the ones in the area that didn't live at the Children's Home. I came up with about 150 children."

Charles' request receives presents galore, enough that every child at the Children's Home, plus those that live nearby, gets something. With a jolly round face that much resembles the one of the man who hands out gifts at Christmas, Charles continues, "Another thing I wanted to do was have lights. Have you ever seen a truck full of lights? I think they shipped me a container of lights like the ones that go on Christmas trees and all of them were tangled. But anyway, we got them and we put them all around Berdzor . . . on the buildings, in the trees, anywhere we could get them off the ground."

"So was there electricity then?" he is asked by one of his listeners.

"We had a generator," he interjects, never missing a beat. "When Christmas came, we hit the switch and everything on the place lit up. You have never seen such excitement." Charles laughs as he continues sharing the memory, which causes him to even more resemble the jolly red-suited fellow with his "Ho-Ho-Ho!"

"There was this village, I guess about twenty miles

away, a lot shorter by the way the crow flies, but it was on another mountain. All these lights flashed on at one time, and along about two o'clock in the morning, here come all these villagers. They thought a space ship had landed and it scared them to death. But they thought they'd better come and pay homage to whatever it was. So there we are, all night long celebrating Christmas, having those villagers and everything. And believe it or not, we had enough gifts to give their children too."

The laughter dissipates into a nostalgic smile as his mind replays all the excitement and episodes of their first Christmas Day in Berdzor in nearly a century. "So that was the first Christmas and I'll never forget what all the kind people in North Carolina did. They sent nice gifts. I remember one little girl got a doll. She'd never seen a doll before. And that little girl . . . tears just rolled down her cheeks. She looked like she was about 12 or 13. I asked if she wanted me to help her open it but she didn't want me to tear the box. She didn't want to mess that box up. It was one of those boxes that had cellophane around the front of it so you could see the doll inside. And she had never gotten anything in her life. She didn't have anything that was hers."

Charles pauses for a moment. One can sense the memories rolling in his head. "I invited the staff over there and they wrapped all those presents, every one of them. And we had a big Christmas tree." There is brief silence. "Some people even sent bicycles. That's one thing that impressed me so much. When I needed something, the people here at home responded."

Christmas is now an annual highlight for the children of Karabakh, and the AGAPE Center is the only place large enough for the community to gather to participate in the greatest celebration of the year. Each January, the children of Berdzor sing and dance and provide a special program or show. They make their own costumes in the sewing classes (with sewing machines, fabrics and sewing materials sent from North Carolina) taught at the Christian Education Center (CEC). Their show—different each year—consist of an array of songs, dances, skits and special programs as children from the Children's Home, the after school classes of the CEC and children of the community all participate in the performance.

Weather is a huge factor as to when the Christmas celebrations happen each year. Although Christmas Day falls on January 6th for them, the Christmas celebration is annually scheduled for sometime between January 13th - 20th, and has been since its start in 1997. Because the only place large enough to hold everyone is the basketball court, outside the AGAPE Center, impassable roads and mountain passes dictate the date. Phones ring continuously in Nara's office on the years when weather prevents the traditional weekend for the event. Because the center offers aid to so many families, a separate day is necessary for the families who live in the villages farther from town and in the border villages. This way they are able to make one long trip for their distribution day, and still pick up the shoeboxes for their children when they make the journey to Berdzor. As with all the distributions, Nara has a card on every family and its members, so she knows each child and each child's situation and thus any specific needs. Also, because there are so many families helped by AGAPE, different villages are set to come on different days to allow a smoother operation for the humanitarian aid distribution and the handing out of the Christmas Shoeboxes.

The 2006 celebration holds a special highlight, thanks to a gift of an accordion from Margaret McCleskey, wife of retired WNCC Bishop Lawrence McCleskey, during her visit to AGAPE that year. All of the singing and dancing is done with the accompaniment of a keyboard *and* the accordion. This is exciting, for the children have an opportunity to experience the music on an instrument that is so much a part of their culture and tradition. Each year's program is followed by party snacks for the children and their parents.

The 2007 Christmas celebration includes several competitions—one for the best singer, the best rhymer and the best dancer. Prizes for these competitions are huge stuffed animals, as large as the youngest children in the orphanage.

The show for 2008 is prepared, as usual, by students of the CEC, the Children's Home and children of the community, but this year it is done in cooperation with a local youth group called "Hayer." (Armenians call themselves "Hay"—an Armenian word. "Er" is the plural suffix, thus "Hayer.") The governor and his wife accept an invitation to participate in this year's celebration. As the event ends, the governor closes with these words: "The USA is big not only with its size and role in the history but more with those who live there, with the true Christians. The sense of our gratitude towards them is as big as their hearts and LOVE, which do not recognize any geographical and political boundaries, it means boundless . . ."

Since 2008, when the idea of Christmas Shoeboxes is implemented into the work of Project AGAPE, each year brings more and more shoeboxes to the Mission Response Center in Terrell, North Carolina. Remember, other humanitarian aid organizations are unable to respond in the disputed territory due to political issues, so the MRC alone is responsible for the distribution of the boxes that are shipped to Armenia. It is amazing how this part of the ministry has mushroomed over the past few years. (A recent trip to Terrell reveals over 2,000 packed shoeboxes sent from just the North Carolina Conference.)

In March of 2009, 379 more Christmas boxes arrive, but too late to be distributed at the Christmas event. Therefore, these boxes are used for the children of the Kashatagh region in March, when the distribution takes place for the villagers. Since they live too far to participate in the Christmas event in January, parents pick up the boxes when they make the trip to Berdzor for their humanitarian aid. Still, it isn't hard to imagine the joy of the children's faces, for that shown on the faces of the parents is one of wondrous excitement.

The 379 boxes mean that 379 village children "were seized with the glow of happiness that day, putting the nice things under their pillows before they sleep, and in the morning those things will be the first things they check to make sure that it was not a dream," one parent later tells.

Another parent shares, "There were so many nice things in an individual box that children were also distributing items to older members of the family, their parents and grandparents."

One mother adds, "And even the plastic boxes are great. We use those as containers to keep different things in the house."

Although the Christmas celebration is a part of the AGAPE tradition since 1997, and there are Christmas boxes for the children of the orphanage (Children's Home) during those years, it is not until 2009 that there is an actual Christmas Shoeboxes distribution for all the children of Kashatagh at the January event. There are 300 children and only 278 individual boxes, so the AGAPE staff quickly pulls some tote bags from a shipment, as well as a few other items to make enough presents for all the participants. During the program, the children involved dance in national costumes, with the best singer and best dancer receiving the biggest Christmas box. Because the event is opened to include Christmas Shoeboxes for all the children, some parents help with the planning of the event. One of the parents, Armen, who plays the keyboard for the event tells, "Only today do we realize that the New Year has come."

After all of the festivities and refreshments each year comes the most exciting part of the day for the children. Father Atanas closes each annual event with words of gratitude "to all those faithful Christians far away who help to fill the hearts of the children with joy and to derive enjoyment from such events, which are occasional in the lives of the children in this region." After a prayer of thankfulness for their brothers and sisters in North Carolina, he moves on to the most pleasant part of his yearly duties – giving Christmas toys to all the children present.

When the last child receives a shoebox, another year

starts for these people "forgotten by the world but living with the struggle for the day to day existence and hoping for better days," thanks to the love of all who support Project AGAPE.

For Charles, that sight of a little girl holding a doll for the first time is a vision still experienced by anyone who helps with the Christmas Shoebox distribution today. The eyes of the children sparkle brighter than any lights on a Christmas tree as the children sense the love that is packed into the shoebox with the other items—socks, a cap or scarf, a toothbrush, suckers, crayons or markers, pens or pencils, a coloring book or tablet, and a toy—age appropriate for each child. Whether you carefully select the items to place in a shoebox and then pack them with love, whether you work at the Mission Response Center to make sure all the boxes have all the necessary and appropriate items and are marked properly for customs clearance, or whether you actually go to Armenia to take part in a distribution of the shoeboxes, you sense a bit of the love that a child feels when they first touch that box, and then open it to enjoy all of its contents. For through that simple act, you *are* the exemplified love of Christ, experienced by each child who receives a Christmas Shoebox.

In the words of Nara, "May the JOY and happy moments of those children, like a boomerang, return back to you."

CHAPTER 19

God's Gift

The Armenian Christmas, which is January 6th, has just passed. The year is 2012 and it is a cold winter's day. There is a knock at the door of the AGAPE Children's Home. At the door stands someone with two children, a boy and a girl. The staff is used to occasionally having people arrive with children, either ones who are the children of two deceased parents, or whose father is deceased and the mother cannot afford to care for them. But there is something different about these two children.

The boy, Pargev, is only 13 months old, the youngest child to ever be brought to the children's home. The age of his older sister, Vartuhi, is not certain and due to her state of malnutrition, it is impossible to determine. They are brought to the home because their mother, only 26, has just died due to heart complications. Both of the children are terribly malnourished, so much so that they are both incredibly small and their health has been affected greatly as a result of their starvation.

There is something really special about this young toddler, Pargev. His name in Armenian means "God's Gift." This new arrival certainly is a gift for all the children of the orphanage. To them, he is like a late Christmas present. They are not used to babies, which he seems to them instead of a toddler, and so they all are excited about him.

Pargev is not nearly as mobile as he should be for a one-year-old. Vartuhi, in addition to not being the size she should be, suffers from both mental and physical development as a result of the malnutrition. It is quite evident that she is nowhere near the same level as the other children. But for now, that doesn't matter. What matters is that the children are shown love and acceptance.

After being first fed and then cleaned and dressed with clean clothes, Vartuhi is surprised with a Christmas Shoebox and she greatly enjoys the presents wrapped neatly inside. It is no doubt the first present she has ever received, and certainly contains the first toys she has ever seen. In fact, these are probably the first things she has ever had that are all her own. She immediately takes all the items from the clear plastic container and begins to play with them. Vartuhi is also given a pair of shoes and clothing.

Pargev is also cleaned and fed and dressed in fresh

clothes. Because there are Christmas Shoeboxes designated for infants, there is a box for him too. Inside are three new diapers, a rattle and a soft toy, as well as a cuddly blanket and a colorful drinking cup.

Now, just over two years later, Vartuhi is so under-developed that at some point, she will likely have to go to a special school in Yerevan that can better assist with her education and her care. But thanks to Project AGAPE she is shown a world of love and a world of hope as new doors open to her.

Pargev is healthy and happy. He still seems like a gift from God to both the other children at the home and to the staff. Watching him grow and develop new skills is most rewarding for them. He brings lots of smiles to the Children's Home as he interacts and plays with the other children. Though still small for his age, the toddler is growing and showing improvements on all levels. Like all of the children at the home, he is extremely well behaved. His presence is still a daily blessing for everyone at the orphanage . . . a gift from God!

CHAPTER 20

The Girls Behind the Wall

The morning begins with an unusual sound, laughter behind the concrete wall that backs up to the outdoor dining hall. It isn't the laughter that is so out of the ordinary, for that is rather predictable, and in fact expected, on the premises of Project AGAPE. There is such camaraderie between visiting workers and the staff that high spirits are typically audible in the air, from sunup to sundown. But this morning, the air sparkles with the frivolous merriment of children. It is clearly not the same afternoon sounds of Dr. Artsakh's grandchildren who habitually visit the playground each evening after dinner. Nor is it the humbled gleefulness heard when the area children receive their Christmas shoeboxes or their school supplies.

A quick glance in the direction of the back concrete wall reveals two capricious girls, one appearing to be a young teen and the other nearing her teen years. Their faces are filled with animation as they actually climb the wall and jump to the ground on the AGAPE side. They are quite at home here so this is obviously not their first visit. Their laughter, its source still unknown, is contagious, as they run across the parking lot to a tree bearing fruit near the front wall.

It soon becomes evident that they are the grand-daughters of Gayane Galstyan, one of the staff persons of Project AGAPE. Gayane—who takes care of everyone's laundry each day, keeps the entire facility clean and helps wherever is necessary—is never seen without a smile on her face. Once the connection is made between the girls and her, it is no wonder the girls are so full of enthusiasm for life.

That zestfulness has not, however, always been the case . . . especially for the older one, Alla, who it is discovered is 15-years-old. Gayane's face, like that of any doting grandparent, beams when she speaks of the two girls. They are clearly a ray of sunshine in her life, even on the bleakest of days.

But then, her face takes on a sorrowfully grim expression as she begins to relay a story that tells of quite a different scene from the one at hand, a scene when even a bleak day would have been a great improvement. "It was 1997. I had lost my husband in the recent war so I decided to move to a small dwelling in Berdzor, the town where my only daughter, Narine, lived with her husband. He, too, had lost his father during that war. Because he was alone there with no family, it was decided that it would be better for the newly married couple to come and stay in my home now that I, too, was in Berdzor.

"Those were extremely difficult times. My son-in-law was a hard worker, but there was no work to be found. He occasionally found an odd job here or there doing minor construction, but nothing permanent."

Gayane looks in the direction of the two girls. "After a year, my first grandchild, Alla, was born. Our living conditions were deplorable. We had no money to buy infant food, which didn't matter, for even if we'd had money, there was no store in Berdzor at that point in time. We were terribly distressed and had no idea what to do. I knew this situation could not continue or the baby would die.

"Out of desperation, I finally went to see the Governor, who had known my husband. I explained our disparity and he promised to find me a job. 'In the meantime, though,' he told me, 'do not let the baby die of malnutrition.' He then advised me to apply to AGAPE for assistance, which I did.

"When I arrived at the office there," Gayane says, the grimness on her face softening into a melancholic wistfulness, "I was met by a young man who informed me that I should speak with the director. He left and a young woman soon returned. As she approached me, all I could do was stare at her. She appeared so young and had obviously not withstood the same trials with which I was dealing. *How can she possibly help me? She will never understand my pain,* I told myself, *or how I feel.* I was so caught up in my own thoughts that I began to feel more distraught. That is until she came closer and I could see into her eyes – eyes that were full of love and understanding and promise. And she had the most compassionate smile on her face. Suddenly all of my apprehension vanished, and I began telling her of my entire life, reluctantly at first. But she sat there listening with such patience and understanding that my words just kept coming as I soon spilled out my entire life, from the difficult days of my childhood that were spent in an orphanage to my appalling current state in Berdzor. It seemed that I had been speaking forever, but still this young woman sat patiently and listened with concern to each word.

"After all that, I still had no clue how to formulate my request. So I finally just blurted out, 'I don't know, will there be someone to help me?'

"The young woman's kind face looked into mine as she answered, 'Don't worry. God is almighty and there will be someone to help you.' She then asked me to wait and she disappeared for a few minutes.

"When she reappeared several minutes later, she was carrying two boxes with all kinds of food and infant formula. My granddaughter was saved."

For a moment, Gayane's words are lost in the background as suddenly the vivacious laughter of Alla takes on the sound of a choir of angels singing of the wondrous works of God. She takes on a totally different appearance as she now portrays a true living miracle, embodied in the shell of a beautiful girl who will all too soon reach womanhood and bear her own family . . . a family that will be part of an on-going miracle, for she clearly possesses a heart of love and a spirit of giving. That trait is obvious now as she picks fruit from the tree and shares it with one of the women of a visiting work team, a sparkling gleam in her eye with each piece of shared fruit.

"I still remember the compassionate smile on that young woman's face." Gayane's words are again audible. "I see it each and every day when I come to work. I see it each time someone in need comes to AGAPE. And I see it even broader when the children and families arrive for either the distribution of Christmas shoeboxes or school supplies, or on the large distribution day when people come with their list of needs and she works so tediously, yet so unwearyingly, to try to find each item needed by each person or family."

Her next words are unnecessary, yet Gayane concludes her story with a huge loving smile of her own. "That young woman was Nara. She was able to find me a job working in the Children's Home prior to my work here at AGAPE. Because my childhood had been spent in an orphanage, that was a perfect place for her to find work for me." She pauses as she looks toward Nara's living quarters. "In all these years of working here, never have I seen that compassion or care absent from her."

Her eyes turn back to the two children running and playing—"happy as two larks," as the expression goes—as they make up their own games and stay occupied. They need no toys, no video games, and they ask for nothing as they enjoy life to its fullest, simply by being a part of God's creation.

"AGAPE saved my granddaughter's life," Gayane concludes. "I do not know what would have happened to my family without their help." She smiles broadly and nods her head. "And now I am able to help my daughter's family thanks to my job at the Berdzor office of Project AGAPE." She goes on to repeat her words of gratitude. "I am so very thankful for all the faithful Christians whose love helped my granddaughter, and my family, to survive through their gifts to Project AGAPE. And their love and support have saved so many lives and helped so many families to make enough money to support themselves and, for some, to help others in the community.

"It is a huge blessing when we are able to reach out and help others by sharing what we have." Her statement speaks volumes as it is amazing to watch the residents of Berdzor and the nearby villages share with their neighbors and help each other, even with what little they have. The love shown through Project AGAPE has set an example that breaks the rule of "What's mine is mine and you can fend for yourself." Beyond the tangible items that have been distributed to the hundreds of families and thousands of residents, AGAPE has given a more valuable lesson – a lesson of selflessness in sharing God's unconditional love, expecting nothing in return.

But this story of Gayane's granddaughters does not end here. It continues, fully demonstrating precisely what Project AGAPE is all about and strives to do. Several days later, as one of the women from the work team takes her daily walk down the steep path from the AGAPE facility, through the town and up the 137 steps to the top of the war memorial, Alla and her younger sister, Gayane (named for her grandmother), follow her. This has become a daily ritual for the trio, for the moment the woman exits the building late each afternoon, after the day's work is complete, the two girls are quickly in step right beside her. It is a touching sight, for one cannot decide whether these girls feel the need to chaperone the woman in a strange land, or whether they simply want to enjoy her company.

It is quickly apparent that this is a joint party, enjoyed by all, as they point to things along the way and teach each other the names for them, the woman in English, the girls in Armenian. There is no doubt it is a fun learning game for the trio. The woman, who has grown accustomed to this habit over the past few days, brings gum or a piece of chocolate each day for the girls. There are always short stops along the way as the girls point out the contents of each store and give a short explanation of it. This is done mostly by pointing to items and in sign language, which has taken on a dialect all its own with their creative motions. Nevertheless, it appears they have grown to understand each other, and more than that, a beautifully tender friendship has developed between them.

This particular day is different though. As they make their usual trek through the town, that is dotted with only a few shops, Gayane (the younger of the two granddaughters) ducks into one of them. She comes out with three ice creams and hands one to the woman. The woman's face is a jumble of emotions as she takes the cone, hesitantly at first, but then with great appreciation at what this young girl has just done. It is a chocolate cone with vanilla and chocolate ice cream on the top. This is a packaged product, from Grand Candy like most of the sweets throughout all of Armenia, for there are definitely no soda fountains or ice cream shops in this place. Yet, from the expression now on the woman's face, it is the most refreshingly delicious ice cream she has ever tasted.

It is easy to see she is fighting tears as she licks the ice cream and the trio makes their way in silence the rest of the way to the war memorial, each of them enjoying the treat provided by the young girl's generosity. There is no doubt the woman wishes she could repay the child, but weighs that as an insult so she graciously and repeatedly says how much she enjoys the cone.

The episode makes the day's excursion to the war memorial more meaningful and intensely more firsthand than usual. For prior to the days that Armenians take back the control of Nagorno-Karabakh from Azerbaijan in the recent war, this is an Azerbaijan monument. Because of that, everything about the monument is styled with half-moon shapes, from the small gardens and wading pools on the way up the steep path to the top step, where there is a large open area with three tall marble sections forming a semi-circle. Khachkars (cross stones) have been added and are now the focal points rather than the small gardens or wading pools. The three tall semi-circle marble walls now contain all the names of the men from this area who were killed during the war, along with a branch to symbolize eternal life. There are so many names that another huge cross-stone with the remaining names now stands to the right of the three columns. It is nearly unfathomable that so many men could be killed in such an unpopulated area, yet at the same time, it demands an astounding admiration for their heroically valiant efforts in trying to reclaim what was once theirs.

That thought is suddenly shattered as the two girls point to a name near the bottom of the left column of this additional stone. They chatter excitedly, trying to grasp the woman's attention until her eyes come to the place where their fingers rest. In their struggle to understand each other, the woman finally comprehends that the girls know this particular name on the monument.

You can literally see the wheels turning in the minds of the two girls as they attempt to find a way to share a thought with the woman. It is finally Alla who remembers the word she has learned at school and blurts out, "Grandfather!"

"This man was your grandfather?" the woman asks, her words reiterated by hand motions.

"Ayo," answer the girls simultaneously, thrilled they have made communication.

"Your grandfather was killed in the Azeri War here?" is the woman's next question.

"Ayo," the affirmative answer comes again as Alla points off in a direction over the mountains.

The woman gives a respectful nod of understanding and sympathy as she looks at the girls in a different light. "Gayane's husband," she says softly to herself while piecing the whole picture together.

"Ayo," the girls confirm in hushed unison. Their faces show the sorrow passed on to them from members of the family who actually knew their grandfather.

The woman looks back at the huge tri-stone wall, this time noticing that each wall also has a Christian symbol or phrase that has been added since Muslim times, such as a leaf, to symbol eternal life. She turns to see the seven khachkars, taking special note of the one with the men's names on it. Her eyes fall again on the one name as she and the two girls embrace in a group hug.

"Common ground," the woman whispers softly as she takes in the panoramic view from the vantage point of where she stands. The entire town can be seen from here, atop this high hill, as well as the roads that lead to Shushi and Stepanakert. Those two words—common ground—however, encompass more than the many miles she can see in all directions from here. They denote the common ground that has been developed in this area through the founding and work of Project AGAPE and the many lives it has touched. "And the examples it has set for all of the children to carry into the next generation," you can almost hear her say as she takes a hand of each girl and they walk back down the steps as a threesome toward the AGAPE complex, the place that has come to be the "common ground" for Kashatagh.

CHAPTER 21

For the Love of a Mother

Boris is 8-years-old and very small for his size due to his malnutrition. His father is dead, a casualty of the recent war. Boris and his small sister, "Little Agnessa," as she is known, live on the street with their mother. Their house has been bombed, and like every other home anywhere remotely close, has been burned totally to the ground destroying what small amount of tangible items they possessed. What food they do find is on the streets, the same as the dogs eat so it is a daily routine of who can get to the crumbs first. Boris' mother is extremely sick from starvation, yet she tries as best she can to hide this from her young children. They are too young to understand anything besides hunger and starvation, for their lives have known nothing different, due to the fall of the Soviet Union and resulting war with Azerbaijan that has robbed them not only of their father but of their home and all of their belongings. In fact, the only life they have known has been extreme poverty, hunger and cold nights on the street – all issues that no one should have to deal with, much less on a continual basis, not to mention their innocent ages.

The mother spends her time trying to find any bit of food for her children, which means she sometimes hides them in a corner of a bombed foundation that is still standing or a place where she knows they will be safe while she looks for any kind of nourishment for them. Because this is their lifestyle, she may sometimes be gone for quite a while until she can return with some morsel to offer them. This habit also allows her to hide the degree of her illness from them.

One day, however, after she has been gone for a few days, Boris leads "Little Agnessa" out of their hiding place to search for their mother. Even in his young mind, he realizes that it is unlike her to be gone and leave them alone at night, especially for this length of time. They set out walking the streets, most of which are in as pitiful a condition as the bombed structures left dotting the countryside. Between gulleys and ruts, chunks of stone and mortar from the debris of a war zone still scattered all over the area, and craters from bombshells, the young pair walk looking in desperation for their mother.

They finally spot her, dead in the street with the

street dogs standing over her and devouring her flesh and bones. Boris manages to finally shoo the dogs away and he and Little Agnessa then sit down beside their mother, keeping vigil over her to keep the animals away. To this day, it is unknown how long they sat there, protecting what was left of the only world they knew and trusted and loved, their mother, until some local police come upon them.

The police, shocked and sorrowful at the sight of finding yet another starved person who has died in the street, a sight that is becoming all too familiar, focus their attention on the two young lives—meager though they are— at hand. Their clothes, tattered and torn and hanging off their bony bodies, are so worn and dirty they no longer have color. There is no telling when their bodies have last been bathed or their hair combed. The condition of the two children, which is nearly as piteous as the sight of their dead and decaying mother, weighs heavily on the hearts of the policemen.

They know there is only one place to take the two starving and desolate children – the AGAPE Children's Home. They know this orphanage is the only place anywhere in the area where Boris and Little Agnessa will, and can, be cared for. Unsure of how many days it has been since the young pair have eaten themselves, the police immediately take them to the home to be cleaned, fed and clothed, and above all else, loved.

Boris adapts to the orphanage much more readily than his sister. The environment, totally new and foreign to them, is filled with laughter and playfulness. It isn't long until he is fully acclimated to being "one of the boys," even though he is much smaller than the others of his age.

For Agnessa, however, the adjustment is much more difficult. She spends her days withdrawn and full of sadness as she sits in the corner, quiet and still with no regards for anyone or any of the activity around her. The teachers and the orphanage staff try diligently to involve her with the other children or to engage her in conversation. Their efforts are fruitless and in vain. They refuse to give up on her as she spends continual hours in silence in the corner, never making even so much as a sound or uttering a whimper. It seems as if her sorrow will never begin to heal.

One day, though, when a team of workers from North Carolina come to the orphanage to spend time and play with the children, their happy and solicitous attitudes fill the place with so much laughter that Agnessa begins to watch the happenings around her. During the course of their visit, she actually smiles. Everyone—from the teachers, the staff, the work team, and especially Boris—is overjoyed to see this for the first time since her arrival at the Children's Home.

Even more surprising for everyone is her readiness to participate in a rhyming game competition at the following Christmas event at the AGAPE Center. She wins, as a result of her good rhyming skills. Her prize is a huge bunny rabbit that is bigger than she, which she immediately accepts and cuddles. The prize for everyone else is the miracle of her transformation as they watch a huge smile cover her entire face and the love show as she clutches and tightly hugs the bunny rabbit. To this day, that prize is continually apparent each and every day as she is eager to participate in everything going on at the Children's Home.

While a recent work team visits the Children's Home, the children are each given a paper that resembles a frame. They are to draw a picture of themselves in the frame. Agnessa, though, decides to draw a picture of one of the visiting team members. Her drawing is complete with the woman's glasses resting on the top of her head, her hairstyle, and even the exact color of her t-shirt along with the English words written on the t-shirt. It is incredibly rewarding to see Agnessa stand with the picture, along with the woman pictured, for a photo. Her face beams.

Agnessa, who is now 13 and growing into a lovely young lady, involves herself in whatever is going on even though she sometimes still stands away from the forefront. She no longer hides in the shadows, though, as she once did. She has a beautiful smile, a smile that masks the ghastly horror of her earliest years. Beautiful dark eyes, thick shoulder-length black hair and a healthy glow on her face give no hint of the pallor once written all over her. Her size is average for her age, especially for a child of this area who has also survived all the devastation and starvation that was her existence for the first formative years of her life.

Boris (pictured in the photo pages, wearing a blue shirt and holding a ball), however, is quite small for his age. Now nearing 18, he is much smaller than even many of the girls at the Children's Home. Happy to be a part of the activities and the daily routine of the orphanage, he generally stands back, carefully assessing each new person who comes to work at or visit the home, finding his own comfort zone with people and any situation before deciding to participate. But he does finally join the group at his own pace and is soon busy doing the same things as everyone else, giving it his very best. And what is most exciting to watch is that Boris is quite proud of his very best, standing tall and upright like a proud peacock with each accomplishment. When Boris smiles—which is rarer than with some of the children—his smile says more of what Project AGAPE has done for him, "Little Agnessa" and all the other children who reside here than words could ever express. It is a smile that will bring any adult to tears, not of what Boris has endured and survived, but at the expressions of love shared with him through AGAPE that have made this smile possible.

The sight of your mother, so sick and malnourished that she dies on the street, with dogs tearing away at her flesh and bones is not a scenario that can ever be forgotten. Neither is the love of people who provide for you . . . your food, your clothing, your shelter, your school supplies and your everyday needs . . . all from people whom you may never meet or even see in photographs. But all of which are gifts of unconditional love that come to Project AGAPE's Children's Home.

CHAPTER 22

The Hen House

It is on a fall afternoon in 2008 when God miraculously guides Nara Melkonyan and Hakob Gumbalyan to a family horribly in need. They are on their way to deliver two bunk beds and mattresses, some food and a huge bag of flour to a family in a Kashatagh village called Aygehovit (meaning garden's valley). Aware that the mother of the family, Heghine Avetisyan, is at the AGAPE Hospital in Berdzor awaiting the birth of her third child, they are taking the supplies to the other two daughters and father so that the items will be available upon the mother's return.

When Nara and Hakob arrive in the village, it turns out that it iSs much harder to find the house of the family than they had expected. They decide to go to the local village school to find the children of the family so that they can give them directions to the house. That way, Hakob can also give the children a ride home. But when they arrive at the school, the children have unfortunately—or so it seems at the time—already left.

Nara and Hakob ask some of the students if they happen to know of the house in question. Gor, a young boy, volunteers that he knows the family and will go with them to the house. He proudly rides in the Dodge truck, undoubtedly enjoying every moment, and takes the pair to their desired destination. The young boy then helps unload everything in the truck and even helps assemble the parts of the bunk beds.

Anna, the older daughter of the Avetisyan family, tells Nara and Hakob that Gor often helps her family, for everyone in her family is female. She goes on to share that Gor sometimes comes during the winter to help them cut firewood, and then helps carry it to their house so they can try to stay warm. He is ever willing to help in any way he can.

When they finish all the work at the Avetisyan dwelling, Nara and Hakob take Gor to his home. It turns out that God has intervened in this mission, for had these two AGAPE personnel not taken this boy home, they would have never found out that his family is living in a hen house. They learn that Alisa, his mother, has four children, the oldest of whom is Gor. She is providing and caring for the family all alone because her husband died in the river a good while before in an effort to make money for the daily bread of his family.

As the story unfolds, it is discovered that the father actually died five years earlier, leaving his wife with four children. He was out fishing one day in the river, having been promised 5000 drams (the equivalent of $10.00) for his day's catch of fish, which is a good amount for a day's work considering the menial average salary is $60.00 per month. It is on that day, though, that he somehow slips and drowns in the river.

Had it not been for Gor being the child who guides Nara and Hakob to the Avetisyan house, they would have never learned of this family's situation. This hen house, in which they have been dwelling for years now, has no windows, nor a normal door. The family immediately becomes one of the main beneficiaries of AGAPE. Their "hen house" is now a more suitable place to live, having been transformed, thanks to the help of the donations sent to the Mission Resource Center and the monetary contributions as well as the love and care of those who serve on work teams.

CHAPTER 23

A Kiss of Gratitude

In order to facilitate all of the people served in the Kashatagh province, Project AGAPE holds a distribution of humanitarian aid in February and March for the families of the villages, many of which are merely 25 or so members of a family living in a cluster. Because the distance they have to travel to Berdzor is so great, and the only path is over bombed roads and weathered paths, it is a difficult journey. Yet because it takes everything they earn from their meager income just to have sustenance of daily bread, these distributions are a welcome event. They come with their list in hand of the number of people in their household and exactly what their needs for simple daily living are. (Remember, the house that holds them is simply a dwelling made from the confines of a bombed or burned shelter that was once a house or an outbuilding.)

The warehouse is well organized so that items can be found quickly and efficiently for the families who come. All distribution is carefully recorded, as to the names of the families and their members—which requires birth certificates for children so that all records are accurate. Nara has a card with each family's name and the number of people in the family along with their ages. This helps the AGAPE staff know many of the needs, and the sizes, for the families from year to year. Recipients have to sign for the gifts, which is an itemized account. All this is necessary for bookkeeping for a humanitarian agency.

Because it is such a great distance for the people to come to AGAPE, without means of travel except walking or the rough village bus, the children do not come, but with the records and birth certificates, Nara and all the staff are able to verify the needs. In addition to the nice warm clothing, hygiene supplies and school supplies, all of which make the recipients extremely happy, Christmas Shoeboxes are given for the children of those who come. Each one who comes has a wish list for additional items they need, such as a blanket, towel or yarn—anything which might help their bleak living condition. It is typically the mother who comes, for in many instances the father was killed in the war, has died from the conditions, or is at home working just so his family can eat.

There is a touching scenario in the February/March

distribution of 2011. Narine Nazaryan, who lives in one of the far away villages and is the mother of five children, comes to receive humanitarian aid. This is the first time she has been to AGAPE for assistance. She is immediately given clothing and Christmas Shoeboxes for all of the children, and then asked what other things her family needs. The staff works eagerly and diligently to help her prepare a wish list of supplies since she has no list. Narine is extremely reserved in making a request for anything and it is quite an ordeal to learn what the family needs.

Nara recalls, "She was very shy and it took us some effort asking questions in different ways to get out of her the names of some things her family needed."

But finally a list is compiled and AGAPE is able to fill every item on the list. As Narine takes the pen to sign for the aid and is still bent over the paper, she wishes to kiss the hand of the person whose hand is outstretched to take back the pen. Although it is a rather awkward situation, it is an exceptionally touching moment.

Narine finally manages to speak. "I don't know how to express my gratitude. I have five children. I haven't told them that I am going to receive some aid. They have always felt bad about that as they don't want anyone in their school to think that because their father has died, their mother has to get aid. Frankly speaking, I don't know what to say to them going back with all these things."

The AGAPE staff advises her to tell the children that all of the items are a Christmas gift, and assure them that they are given for everyone regardless of their social conditions. With those words of encouragement, Narine thanks everyone at the distribution warehouse and leaves for the long return to her village.

No one can believe it when, on the very next day, Narine makes the long journey again across the horribly rough roads on the village bus just to bring a letter of gratitude back to the AGAPE Center. The letter reads:

About ten years after the earthquake of 1988, on January 22, 1999, without having elementary means for existence, we moved from Spitak and resettled in the Dzorap village of Kashatagh region of Karabagh. My fourth and fifth children were born here. It was hard to raise and feed our five children. But my husband and I worked hard to "squeeze bread out of stone" and sustain our family. Unfortunately, the inexorable fate hit me hard again: all of a sudden my husband died leaving the care for the children on my shoulders. Our older son will be drafted to the army soon, and the young son is only eight years old. Four of my children are students. Your organization supported me as mother of many children, and I express my deep gratitude for that. I was frank and told my children everything including how well I was accepted here and what a great support I received. They were very touched and asked to write this letter on their behalf as well. Again and again, our deepest gratitude to all the people in the far country stretching the helping hand to our family, giving their love and bringing hope to us. I don't feel desperately lonely in my troubles any more. God bless them all . . .

CHAPTER 24

". . . Then Feed Just One"

There is a famous quote by Mother Teresa, "If you can't feed a hundred people, then just feed one." Those well-known words are what immediately come to mind when one learns of the countless instances of malnutrition and deaths from hunger brought about by the triple whammy of catastrophic events that shattered the economy of Armenia, particularly Nagorno-Karabakh. Many strides have been made to help numerous families during the 20-year tenure of Project AGAPE, yet there are still heart-wrenching accounts of starving families encountered by the

AGAPE staff. One of the most upsetting instances of the past several years is one from February of 2006.

The AGAPE staff is on their way from the Yerevan office to Berdzor for the winter distribution for families when they hear about a newborn child who has died due to malnutrition. In order to verify the hearsay, they call the AGAPE Hospital to check on the baby's death. They are relieved to learn that the deceased infant's mother and one of her children have been saved by the doctors and are already on their way home, back to the village of Dzorap. However, the doctors also share some gruesome details that shed light on the macabre living conditions of the family.

The father, who is an Azeri War veteran, suffered a concussion that left him with injuries to the brain making him unable to work and provide for his family. Therefore the mother of the child had nothing to eat, so consequently there was no milk to feed the child. She arrives at the hospital with the two youngest of her three children, and although every effort is made to save the lives of the two hospitalized children, all attempts to save the newborn child are useless. A post-mortem examination shows that other than starvation, the newborn was extremely healthy. There was no other reason for the death except that the stomach was filled with . . . air. The other child, who is so affected by malnutrition, suffers tremors and shakes uncontrollably. Doctors at the hospital, however, succeed in at least saving the life of this child.

Immediately the AGAPE staff purchases 110 pounds of flour and several other staple food items for the family. They also go to the warehouse to gather blankets, new pillows, new shoes and clothing for both the children and the parents and then go to visit the family. The mother's condition is one of total despair and desperation. As Nara speaks to her, the mother is exceedingly thankful. But her sorrow sounds forth as the only words she can find are, "Even golden palaces will not replace my child's life. My Sun (the newborn child's name was Arevik, which in Armenian means, small sun) became dim. But I am very grateful for your help, for it will help my other two children."

The gifts of love are unloaded and as young Aram glimpses the food and new shoes, happiness partially lights up his face. Yet the mournfulness in his eyes, combined with the lamentation of his whole body language, is still present as he thinks of leaving his dead sibling behind in Berdzor. Still, it is encouraging to see him try one pair of shoes after another until he discovers just the right size for his small feet.

After all of the articles of clothing and household items are distributed to the family, and the mother is given some financial aid, the AGAPE staff is curious about the living conditions of the house. What they find is worse than what they have imagined. They tremble in horror as they enter the one small room where the family is living, cramped beyond words. Even as tiny as their abode is, there is still a window-size crack in one of the walls. The floor is terribly damp, with small pools of water in some spots. The walls are no more than a "pattern" of stones with huge gaping holes between them. In fact, it is an effort to even call them "walls." Several large stones are on top of the flat roof, protecting what materials do cover the dwelling from being blown away by wind. There is no way to paint a picture that adequately reflects the harrowing vision in front of their eyes. It is a shocking reminder that this woeful situation is the same for the majority of families in these remote villages of Kashatagh, which are far from Berdzor and the AGAPE Center.

Even worse, it is a stark reality that there is NO other organized means of help for these families besides Project AGAPE, who is a friend to them as it strives to change—and even save—lives. It is only through the love and dedication of Christians who contribute to this worthy project that any change can happen in this corner of the world (part of the oldest Christian nation in the world) that has been totally forgotten, or is completely inaccessible, by others. Yet this is an area of the world that needs the most help. For most living in these areas, AGAPE is the only "sun" they see, and as small as that sun may seem, it is alive and productive, unlike little Arevik.

When the mother is asked why she did not request assistance earlier, the AGAPE staff discovers that the family recently moved to the Dzorap village from one of the faraway villages of Goris, a fairly large town and the last one of any size in Armenia before crossing the border into Nagorno-Karabakh. Sadly, because they are newcomers to the area, they are unaware of AGAPE until this tragedy and the staff comes to visit them.

Another sad fact is that very few people around the world are aware of Project AGAPE and the impact it has on the many residents of Nagorno-Karabakh. Or of the change that can be made possible for these people, some of the neediest who have miraculously survived a slate of some of the most unbearable atrocities of the world, through even the smallest of contributions. There is an Armenian expression, "Tsavd tanem," which translated means, "Let me take your pain." Although there is no such saying in English, it has not kept supporters of Project AGAPE from "feeding just one" or sharing the pain of their Armenian brothers and sisters through the love shown to them. The result is a rejoicing of the blessings of God's love, AGAPE love, which is helping to make the sun shine brighter in Nagorno-Karabakh.

CHAPTER 25

Building Bridges

One of the longtime goals of Project AGAPE is the renovation of houses in the community surrounding Berdzor. The first immediate need, however, is the repair of the Children's Home. Upon completion of the final phase of that project—the laundry room—in June of 2008, all thoughts turn to renovating the community houses. That poses a huge problem though. The majority of houses in the area are in such bad condition that they can "hardly be defined as shelters suitable for human beings."

Therefore, once a decision is finalized to begin these

renovations, the hardest work begins, and that is trying to determine who is the neediest among the needy. It is a dreadfully painstaking assessment to choose one dwelling to be first. However, the decision is finally made and the Robert Matinyan family is chosen for the first project.

There are ten extended members of the Matinyan family living under one roof—if one can consciously call it a roof. Robert, his wife Karine, and two married sons with their families all live in one room. Arman, the younger of the two married sons, has three children, two of which are twins. One of the twins dies as a result of the deplorable conditions. Tigran, the oldest son of Arman, has undergone heart surgery, again caused by the appalling environment of the "house." All of the children suffer from heart issues, aggravated by the living situation.

The Project AGAPE staff is excited to inform the family that their dwelling is the first one chosen for repairs and that renovation will soon begin. Yet they are taken back a bit at the indifference shown by the Matinyan family. "We thought it was just another promise like we had heard from others for the past 14 years, though an inner voice told us that AGAPE never gives promises without keeping those." Their statement is quite a tribute to the work and the reputation of Project AGAPE and what they are, and have been, to the area.

Still, it is not until tons of cement and all the other necessary construction materials arrive at that house that joyful smiles light up the ten faces that have before been filled with hopelessness. The AGAPE staff works alongside a mason, hired from the Kashatagh area to help support yet another family with some means of income. Their tirelessness and concentrated efforts soon transform the ruins of a warzone into a building suitable for the entire family. All that is lacking is a roof, which will soon be constructed by a team of workers from the Western North Carolina Conference of The United Methodist Church.

One of the most amazing sights of the entire process is the animated faces of the neighborhood children, thrilled to be a part of the work as they carry the water needed for mixing the concrete. Because the only water source is a long distance from the house, they look like little ants working so hard in their persistence. They are eager and proud to be a part of this "first family" experience.

Almost all of the necessary work is completed and the only thing that waits is the arrival of the work team who will assemble and erect the roof. They arrive in July, right on schedule to start where the AGAPE staff and mason have left off, making all the essential preparations for the team to finish the renovations. There are 14 people who work hard, fast and furiously in the short span of a few days to give the Matinyans' house the last of its facelift. They are meticulous in making sure the roof is sturdy and will last for a long time.

The visible change in the structure is almost inconceivable as it is transformed into a remarkable spectacle to behold. The most beautiful sight, though, is invisible. It is the bridge that had been constructed between the work team and the community. This bridge is strong and everlasting. The team offers Christian love and dedication to the family, which is eagerly accepted. In return, the family offers Christian hospitality by sharing what little they have with the team.

Another interesting aspect of the renovation is how not only the Matinyan family, but also their relatives and adults and children from the community help as much as they are able with the house. But even more than that, they seek to engage one of the team members, if there is one taking a break for a moment, to speak with or to show pictures they have painted or treasured items they have managed to hold onto. One of the most extraordinary instances of this is when Karine brings out a 100-year-old prayer book that she has inherited from her ancestors, along with several pictures painted by her sister.

An environment so contaminated that it causes illness and death is replaced by clean, fresh air that is now permeated only with the radiation of warmth and love, shared by all who participated in any way in the renovation. The gratitude of the family overflows as they express their deepest and most heartfelt appreciation to all of the team, and also to all who donated money to help with the project. In their words, "We wouldn't be able to rebuild those ruins and have a warm house even till the end of our lives if not for your help and Christian love. You are real Christians." Karine, her eyes filled with tears, keeps reiterating that statement over and over to the team.

When the work is finally completed, the time for farewell is painfully sad and brings many tears, both from members of the family and the work team. Their time together has been more wonderful than any of them could have ever imagined, and for the work team members, a

meaningful experience second to none. The lasting sentiment, one that will be forever remembered by both the
Matinyan family and the members of the work team from
Western North Carolina, is "Don't be sad because it's over,
smile because it happened . . ."

CHAPTER 26

"Happiness . . ."

It is 2009, and the AGAPE staff is again faced with the issue of determining which two families are the neediest of the needy when it comes to the matter of house renovation. As in 2008, when the house renovation project is begun, they find this to be an intensely arduous task. Therefore, they resolve to approach the governor of Kashatagh for his assistance in suggesting five families from which to choose, especially now that governmental assistance is available to help with the renovation of houses in the Berdzor area. Their request is granted, and with that comes a list of five families whose "houses"—most of whose present conditions do not even meet the criteria for the definition of a house—are of immediate consideration. The AGAPE staff, now with a much smaller base from which to choose, tackles the difficult task of naming "the neediest of the needy."

They are ecstatic when they see that one of the names is that of Valerik Avanesyan. This family, one of the largest refugee families in Berdzor, is no stranger to AGAPE. Their native home is the village of Maragha, in the Mardakert district of Nagorno-Karabakh, but because that area is controlled by the neighboring country when the war with Azerbaijan begins, they seek refuge in the Kashatagh district. Since the very first years of charitable activity in this area, AGAPE has been helping this family.

When they first come to Berdzor, there are twelve members of the Avanesyan family. Because AGAPE keeps immaculately detailed documentation for all distributions, the AGAPE staff is aware of all the happy marriages of Valerik's daughters and births of his grandchildren, as well as the sad death of his mother—all occurrences that happen since their move to Karabakh. Each distribution brings an update on their family card, which is followed by special gifts or condolences. So naturally when Valerik's name appears on the governor's list, the AGAPE staff loses no time in exploring the possibilities for renovations on their current dwelling. Aware that a building team is coming in June, they want to be sure everything is ready and in order for the work to make their "house" a home.

There are no words to describe the happiness exhibited by the Avanesyan family when they are notified that they are going to be the recipient of housing assistance. "You don't know what this means for me," Valerik expresses emotionally. "I am now sick and may not live long, but now

I know I will not die without seeing this house repaired. My sons have not married because they are ashamed to marry and bring someone into such conditions as we have. They are concerned of how life would be for their family members, for we have experienced what it means living in a wet house with a roof hanging over your head like a Damocles' Sword."

When the staff first examines the roof, its support system seems to be adequate, so that only the rusty tin requires replacement. It is not until the AGAPE staff, with the help of Valerik's two sons, removes the old tin that they fully understand, firsthand and almost a little too personal, what was meant by the term "Damocles' Sword." As they begin to remove the tin, the entire wooden skeleton of the roof caves in, collapsing all around them into nothing but splinters and useless sticks of wood good for nothing now besides firewood. What was seemingly a decent construction now, in its absence, shows all the wounds of the house.

A mason is hired to rebuild walls that are either long gone or a product of the fall of "Damocles' Sword." It takes several days, but soon a new bond-beam is constructed for the roof and the walls are made level so that a work team can come in and finish making this a safe house rather than a wet house. The team arrives during the next couple of weeks and under the direction of two skilled leaders, both of whom have worked on AGAPE projects in the past, reconstruction is completed on Valerik's house (called the Hospital House due to its proximity to the AGAPE Hospital in Karabakh) and another house (called the Church House due to its proximity to the newly constructed church in Berdzor). Arman, a man who suffers from heart problems and who lives in a house renovated the year before, also comes to help. His spirit exemplifies the willingness of the Armenians to reach out to their brothers and sisters, to take what little they have—whether it be in the form of helping hands, food or possessions— and share it. Needless to say, the morale of all involved is high as they together offer a better way of life to a family.

In any project, it is amazing what can be accomplished as each person brings his or her gifts "to the table" and unite as one. As each person does what he or she can manage, it seems they miraculously wind up being capable of actually doing more. Women and teens carry heavy stones for the walls and wood for the roof structure. Men labor alongside the professional carpenters and builders on the team, who are working wonders from high on the roof. Together they see a change happen right before their very eyes as a house appears where only stones and a pile of sticks lay prior to their arrival. This is a living example of following Christ's greatest commandment, "Love your neighbor as yourself." That love is shown through helping those who are desperately in need. This is true whether in Armenia, another needy country or at home. Working together as God's hands builds a camaraderie that is unexplainable. Any time God's love is at the center of any task or project, wonderful things happen.

There is only one way to describe the overwhelming emotion felt by both the Avanesyan family and the workers of the team who serve alongside Valerik during this amazing transformation process of his house; a house that now literally meets all criteria for the definition of the word. As Henry Drummond said, "Happiness . . . consists in giving, and in serving others."

The second house selected for renovation belongs to Tamara Avetikyan. She is well known by the AGAPE staff for she miraculously manages to raise her only son alone during the dark and seemingly hopeless years that many suspect will never end. Her son, Artak, finally finds the courage to marry even though they live in such a small hen house. Old rusted sheets of tin barely provide a roof over the walls, none of which are exterior, but only adjoining walls of an interior frame of what had once served as a house only large enough for chickens.

It is in this house that Artak and his wife are raising their first child. At the time the AGAPE staff visits to evaluate the house for renovations, they learn his wife has only been home ten days with their second child. The ghastly condition of Tamara's dwelling brings great joy to the staff when they realize that they will be able to help this family. Yet the face of Tamara is unchanged, marred by a gloomy expression caused by such long severe years of trying to raise a son in this environment. The staff prays that the renovation will take away some of her sorrow.

In order for the house to be ready for the Western North Carolina building team when it arrives, much groundwork is necessary. As it is, there is not even a base on which the team can begin work. Artak works with the

AGAPE staff to remove the old rusty sheets of tin from the roof so that a mason can construct some walls and a band beam to which a new roof can be attached. A great obstacle arises due to the lack of water near the house. The mason is unable to prepare the necessary cement to do his work.

The mayor, who was the head of the construction department for this Kashatagh administration before being elected a mayor, is called to help get water to the location. That is when they learn that water is not the real obstacle. It so happens that the house sits right on the edge of a hill at the highway. Years of rain have eroded the soil around it so that there is now a great possibility that the "hen house" will wash away if a heavy rain comes. The mayor's professional advice is not to spend a cent on a house; it will most likely be worthless before much longer. "Your work will most probably be in vain if AGAPE continues with the renovation project," he shares with Nara.

As she and the staff go to deliver the bad news, fearing this will cause Tamara to become even more downcast, they happen to see a house through the trees that is up another hill. "Who owns that house?" they ask Tamara and Artak. No one seems to know.

The AGAPE staff walks up the hill to the house and knocks on the door. No one answers so they go back to the mayor's office, sure he will know who owns it. As predicted, he is the source of information. He makes one call and immediately is able to shed light on what had moments earlier seemed a dead-end situation. "No one owns the house," he tells them when he gets off the phone.

Immediately Nara and the AGAPE staff request that

he grant the vacant house to Tamara and her family. The mayor receives the request favorably. A contract is signed between the mayor's office and Project AGAPE, enabling AGAPE to begin immediate renovation on it. Within a couple of days the staff, along with Artak and the mason, begin work on the family's new house, no longer the size of a hen house.

The situation proves to be an important lesson for all involved as it also gives a reason for a smile to appear on Tamara's face. They all discover that it is God's hand in all the obstacles, and that when a wall of desperation stands in the way, an invisible miraculous hand demolishes it.

A second team, which arrives simultaneously with the first team, gets to work on the "new" house, referred to as the Church House. As with the team who works on Valerik's house, there is an abundance of energy and enthusiasm as the second team gets busy creating a livable dwelling for Tamara's family. Arman proves to be a voice of encouragement for this team and family as well as he pitches in to do what he can.

The happiness for all of the missioners continues for, once both houses are renovated, they break into groups, one of which visits the AGAPE Children's Home teaches the children painting skills. Another small group, whose members possess medical skills, visit the villages to help the hospital personnel. The happiness—as quoted by Drummond—continues to spread, not only for the ones receiving an abundance of help and friendship, but also for those who are helping and serving.

Chapter 27

Giving Back

The year is 1995 and the AGAPE Children's Home in Berdzor has just recently been launched. Nine-year-old Ella Khachatryan is one of the first residents who comes to the home for shelter and care. She, like half of the other children at the orphanage, is a one-sided orphan. Her father is killed in the Azeri War and her mother, having absolutely no means of support, is unable to provide any type of existence for her two daughters.

There is no other place for Ella and her sister to go besides the Children's Home. Once there, they receive sufficient food, clothes, a clean and healthy environment in which to live, and most of all, loving care. It is their first, and actually only, promise of hope following the arduous living situations that result from the combination of the earthquake, the Azeri War and all of the political and economic crises that rip at Armenia during that point in time.

Ella's story is like so many others who have found a chance at life thanks to Project AGAPE and all those who support it. Since its beginning in 1995, the Children's Home still holds its place as one of the most invaluable services of this mission project. It continues to be recognized as a symbol of generosity, compassion and hope for children not only of the Berdzor region but all of Kashatagh, as it has for hundreds of children during the past nearly two decades.

Children of the orphanage receive an excellent education, and many of them continue their education in universities or have gone on for specialized training to prepare them for particular professions. For Ella, though, her decision is to stay on and work at the Children's Home to care for the children who come to live there. She realizes it is only because of people who cared for her when she was a child that she is even alive today. Her ambition is to give that same chance at life to others.

Ella's message to the supporters of Project AGAPE and those who support missions is that it is only through the generosity and love of concerned people like YOU that she is able to care about other children of today's world and supplement the lack of love they have to endure in their own young lives. "Besides," she asks, "who will care about orphans better than an orphan?"

This story of paying back is only one of several

shared by former residents of the AGAPE Children's Home. They are so appreciative of how this opportunity saved their lives that they wish to offer the same opportunity to others. In addition to that, it is heartwarming to realize the number of mothers who have been given a job at the orphanage to be able to have means to care for their own children, as well as giving hope to children who have lost both parents.

The Children's Home is one of the most important branches of the services of Project AGAPE. It is no wonder that it was one of the first endeavors for improvements in the Kashatagh province of Nagorno-Karabakh. Many lives have been saved, and forever changed, due to the work of those who have invested time, energy and money in the Children's Home. Lives not only of the children who reside—or have resided—there, but parents with deceased spouses who have been able to deal with life easier thanks to the comfort of knowing their children were given an abundance of care in the midst of such an otherwise dismal situation.

CHAPTER 28

School Days

The Kashatagh district may be needy in most every area, but there is one area in which they could teach many other places a lesson or two. That is in the area of education. Though there is a huge need for supplies for the two schools of Berdzor, supplies that are provided by donations sent to Project AGAPE, these schools are at the top of the proverbial totem pole when it comes to the actual education being received by the students. The entire region is below poverty level, but they are rich in discipline and instruction. Their literacy rate is 99.6%, placing them 19th out of

196 countries. To better understand the value of the support of Project AGAPE to these students, it is imperative that one thoroughly understands the immense value of education in such a down-trodden area.

First and foremost, it is important the reader understands that the local administration of Kashatagh is responsible for the schools, not Project AGAPE. Unlike the emergent customs clearance system, Armenia and Nagorno-Karabakh have a very well developed educational system; "the only good thing," some would say, inherited from the Soviet time. Of all the republics in the Soviet education system, Armenia is the most successful because of the traditionally great value education holds in Armenian culture. This system—"already created of good soil," as it is described—is governed by the Ministry of Education and Science in both Armenia and Karabakh.

There are two schools in the Berdzor area, School #1 and School #2. They are numbered chronologically in the order in which they were reconstructed since both were bombed and burned to the ground during the war. Though the facilities themselves are quite primitive, the students certainly do not lack in instruction. School #1, which is up the mountain behind the Project AGAPE facility, is attended by the children who live on the mountainside as well as those of the Children's Home. School #2 is down the mountain and attended by students in town.

Though the administration is in charge of the schools, the success of the schools and the students' ability to learn is directly dependent on Project AGAPE. When asked if the donation of school supplies is the project's "only" contribution toward the education of the Kashatagh children, Nara is quick to respond. "There isn't any child in those two schools that was grown without AGAPE's help. First of all, most of them were born in the AGAPE Hospital. Assistance from the project was very comprehensive help: starting from shoes, socks, clothing and winter coats, educational supplies and hygiene supplies. The schools received all kinds of help with supplies to get started (sewing materials, sewing machines, maps, books, desks, blackboards).

"It is only recently that School #1 has begun to teach music, art and sports. For many years, the AGAPE Christian Education Center was the only place in Berdzor where children could receive that kind of after-school education, such as chess, art and music. Because of the classes we offered, and continue to offer, classes in computer skills, English language, chess, dancing, carving, painting, sewing, sports and many other classes and activities, many of our students went on to become teachers and offer instruction in this same Christian Education Center. Others went on to become students in the universities of Yerevan and Stepanakert. One of them, Varuzhan Geghamyan, is now doing research at St. Petersburg University in Russia.

"As with the story of Varuzhan, the lives of all the children in these two schools is so interwoven—and continues to be—with the history and activities of Project AGAPE, that the word 'only' is not relevant as to what support they get from the project. All of the students come from families involved in our Cattle Project, House Renovation and other projects. Even the sports and cultural events taking place in those two schools would not be possible without the necessary supplies that they have received and continue to receive from Project AGAPE, like t-shirts, socks, sport shoes for sport events and sewing supplies and sewing machines for their cultural events." Her words are immediately understood for these students have even won awards in national competitions with the dramas, art and dancing they have learned through the Christian Education Center, wearing the costumes they have made themselves from the fabrics, sewing materials and sewing machines supplied to the center by Project AGAPE." One student who excelled in acting and dance is now at a university studying to become a movie director thanks to the help and education she received through the project.

Success stories such as these paint the scene of the significant importance of Project AGAPE to the education, both creatively and intellectually, of the children of Karabakh, particularly in the Kashatagh region. And it all comes from materials donated by the hands of the United Methodists of North Carolina, and other contributors who have become active in the mission of showing love . . . a love that overcomes violence. It is the living out of the reality of the love exemplified through the resurrection.

Nara mentions another important aspect of Project AGAPE's influence on education, one probably rarely considered, and that is education personified. "There is a very rare opportunity in Armenia and Karabagh for the students to experience hearing and learning the spoken English through the team members. This is a lesson they cannot attain at the school."

Her comments are verified by Hakob Hakobyan when he pays a visit to the AGAPE Center. Hakobyan (which he is called in this chapter to alleviate confusion with Hakob Gumbalyan, the AGAPE staff member) is a masterful leader who demonstrates a wealth of knowledge and experience in the field of education, both in instruction and the psychology of education. It is obvious in speaking with him that he is highly educated and also that his command of the English language is exceptional. Given his appearance and demeanor, it makes one wonder whether he is from the area.

Nara, in her introduction of him, clarifies that speculation. "He was the assistant director of the Christian Education Center when he first came here, but now he is the Director of School #2. I believe that experience helped him with this new position. He did an excellent job with the Christian Education Center, but lack of funding meant we had to close the center for a brief period last year. So he has close ties to Project AGAPE."

One of the work team members asks Hakobyan about the school, how long he has been here and what particular needs the school and the children have. He sits for a moment, clearly putting his thoughts together before slowly proceeding; his English perfect as he is deliberate in his speech. Open and frank about the exact details of his coming to Berdzor, and equally appreciative of the American's eagerness to find ways to help the students, he begins, "I spent ten years in Yerevan as a teacher, and have now been here ten years. When I came here in 2004, I worked at the School #2, where I taught English. I was also the Assistant Director for Project AGAPE's Christian Education Center. I am now the Director/Principal at School #2 for grades 1 – 12, where I also teach English."

His dialogue picks up speed and intensity as he continues to speak. Hakobyan is clearly in his element, so much so that you can hear the passion in his voice as he discusses the education of his students. "There are approximately 180 students enrolled in the school currently. They come back on September 1st, so we will get an accurate count for this year on that date. We never know who is coming back until school actually starts. Each year produces more students as the population here grows.

"Ninety percent of our students go on to college. All of the students who graduated this past year are going to college. My daughter is one of those students." Hakobyan is literally beaming with this announcement.

"Are the students required to get their own supplies, or does the school provide them?" The worker's question stems from Soviet times and the desire to know if the practice from then, of supplying all of a student's supplies, still holds true.

"We provide all the books that the students use at school, and they are turned in at the end of each school year. With regards to the other supplies, we are very dependent on donations, from places like your own state. As you can imagine, there is always a great need. But we give them copy books," he continues, pointing to a writing tablet lying on the patio table, which is currently serving as AGAPE's conference table. It is one of the sturdy-backed composition books without spirals. "Small ones or big ones, it doesn't matter. But **not** the loose paper. We only use this style of copy books. And of course we also need construction paper, pens and pencils, and colored pencils," he adds as an afterthought. Hakobyan then thanks the team member profusely for the work of the entire mission team, and for the many ways the people of North Carolina are helping the school children with their donations of the necessary school supplies through Project AGAPE.

"What about computers? Do you have computers at the school?" he is asked.

"We have one computer classroom with eleven computers. It is a new class, with one teacher for all the students. During their computer lessons, every class goes to the computer room and learns, with the help of the teacher. Of course there are no computers in any of the homes so this is the only chance the children get to use them, but they are quick to learn and are doing amazingly well."

Talk then changes to the reason Hakobyan has chosen today to visit. It is important to note here that one thing is quickly perceived in watching the activity at Project AGAPE, at least during the summer months. The outdoors of the facility is where most of the meetings with recipients of the project's support take place. In America, there is a saying, "Most business transactions happen on the golf course." The same could be said here, except instead of a golf course, most meetings happen outside Nara's office under a makeshift patio, the same one where meals are served for the staff and the work teams. Perhaps that is so everyone can enjoy the fresh air, the breeze and the spectacular mountainous view; perhaps so the always-present hospitality can be shown at the table with the serving of thick, strong coffee, which is a staple of Armenian culture.

Nara sends a staff person to retrieve something in the distribution center. The staffer quickly returns with a large brown pasteboard box marked "School Supplies" on the top. It is noteworthy that the words are in English, obviously marked before the box left America.

Hakobyan quickly opens the box and is like a child at Christmas when he sees it filled with plastic binders. Being that all schools begin in Armenia on September 1st and it is presently the middle of August, time is at hand. *And Nara's hand seems to be the one that matters at the moment*, one would quickly assess, noting all the many other visits she's had during the week.

Nara has a reputation, due to countless stories of volunteers in mission and also those who have worked with her in America. Everyone speaks of how much she is able to accomplish with so little, and of how carefully she protects the funds to get the most possible from them. Seeing her in action with the distribution of donated materials is living evidence of that. Her reputation is well earned.

Content that his needs will be met for the school and that necessary supplies for the students will follow, thanks to Project AGAPE, Hakobyan finishes his coffee and says his good-byes. He then leaves to prepare for a new year of instruction, the brown pasteboard box in tow, but not without first extending an invitation to any interested team members to visit School #2 and see firsthand what the education system is like in this disputed territory.

"Education has always been first and foremost in

our Armenian culture," Nara explains after his visit. "To tell you how important it is, every school in Spitak was destroyed after the earthquake there in 1988. It was devastating for 25,000 people were killed . . . men, women and children." As she speaks, her sorrow over the event is still evident in her face and the pity still sounds in her voice. "There were 4,000 killed in just one town. Even after that, and the total mass destruction, the surviving children had school as much as possible. They kept going, sitting on rocks outside to continue their education. That was the most pitiful situation of all. When workers began to come from North Carolina after Project AGAPE was started, a team from Western North Carolina helped rebuild the only school in service again at that time."

Her comment reiterates an experience shared by one of the women from a Western North Carolina work team who has just returned home, and who has served on several trips to Armenia. "When we arrived, the children were meeting in sections of old shipping containers we had sent. It was freezing inside them. There was some sort of small heater in the middle of the classroom that was putting out so much smoke and soot that it was a wonder the children could breathe. You could not even see your hand out in front of your face, yet those children were there—still in the uniforms or same clothes they could find after the earthquake—working and learning under the tutelage of a dedicated teacher. That poor teacher could barely make out the students in front of her.

"That's when we realized how great the need was for a school so the conference, and some of the supporting churches of Project AGAPE, raised money to build a school and improve the learning conditions for the children of the Spitak area. It was difficult to work there amidst all the rubble still left and the number of tombstones on the mounds surrounding the area, especially with the beautifully etched photographs of the children on the tombstones."

The visit to School #2, a couple of days later, proves to be even more enlightening than the earlier conversation with Habokyan. From the first step inside the front door, life abounds with greenery and plants. "This building was an old school in ruins, I would say, all without floors when I first arrived here." He is quick to add, "Like everything else here, it had been bombed and burned terribly, but when this is all one has, one makes the best of it and moves forward rather than moan about what he or she does not have." The visitors have taken merely one step inside the structure and already they've been taught an invaluable lesson from this man, not only about education, but of life in general. His comment says much about why Project AGAPE is so successful; perhaps those skeptics who only gave the project five years at the outset were thinking from their perspective and not that of the Armenians, particularly the ones who live in Nagorno-Karabakh.

As the visitors enter the school, Hakobyan is quick to point out the saying written on the outside of the door leading from the landing into the main body of the school. Translating the words, he reads, "Here it is written, 'No entry without a smile!' This was the students' idea and the fifth graders wrote it. They remind each other of it, if need be, but that is a rarity." That, in itself, opens the door for a healthy learning environment.

Directly across the hallway is a portrayal of Saint Mesrop Mashtots (who invented the Armenian alphabet in 405 AD), holding a large stone tablet, similar to the one often pictured with the Ten Commandments. Again, Hakobyan translates the words inscribed on it, "'To know wisdom and instruction; to perceive the words of understanding.'"

These words, translated from Solomon's *Book of Proverbs*, are reputed to be the first sentence ever to be written in Armenian by Mashtots. They hold great prominence in their ideology of education, as well as of life in general. Likewise, Mashtots holds a major position in their fields of education, history and culture and is known to students from the earliest age. Their alphabet, which originally consisted of 36 letters, now contains 39 letters, all of which have a beautifully artistic quality about them.

From the live plants, the positive attitude and the importance of wisdom, instruction and understanding displayed, the atmosphere presented for the students creates an aura that is conducive to learning from the moment they enter the front door. That characteristic tone only increases as one proceeds to the classrooms. One of the first things you notice as you walk into the hallway is how exceptionally clean and spotless everything is. The floor's coating of polyurethane makes it look as if it has been spit-shined. Everything inside the classrooms is primitive. The old wooden desks seat two students at each one. Rooms are heated by radiators. Light bulbs hang by a wire from the ceiling. The teacher's desk is barely larger than a student's desk in the States. It is amazing how neat and tidy everything is, and organization is paramount. That is obvious from the orderly conditions of every single classroom. It is no wonder there is such a high literacy rate and respect for education.

Hakobyan, aware of the visitors' comments, states, "Cleanliness, tidiness is the first thing. One cannot learn in a situation of clutter. Organization and openness is key." That is not only the way it is in school here; that principle pervades throughout the entire country.

Each classroom has a wall with a small chalkboard, a wooden dowel for a pointer, and an old washcloth or rag, albeit immaculately clean, hanging on a nail beside the chalkboard to clean the board. The boards in the first and second grade classrooms have lines as guides for handwriting, and judging from the samples remaining in a folder on the teacher's desk from the previous school year, their penmanship is remarkable with perfectly formed letters.

"Because we do not have resources in the ground, our only defense is our minds. Therefore, we begin scientific and engineering skills in the fifth grade," Hakobyan goes on to explain." The unseen and unspoken factor that slowly becomes obvious is that there has to be teachers qualified to offer this elite kind of instruction. Teachers who, like this individual, are willing to live here for the sake of the Armenian children and families either left be-hind following the Azeri War or who have come to help populate the area in support of those who fought so bravely to regain what had originally been their homeland.

As with the poster of Mashtots greeting students downstairs, there are two pictures—one of Mary holding the Christ-child and another of Christ as a man—that greet students as they reach the top of the stairs on the second floor. Underneath them is written "Like your friend as you would like yourself." Hakobyan shares that the students also wrote this on the wall, choosing it to be their attitude about how to treat others at school. "And if there is a prob-lem with that, the students handle it so there becomes no discipline problem." He goes on to explain that they do not include religion as a class, yet it is certainly a part of their life. "In fact, the Christian history and heritage is a part of the education of the students. This is, after all, the oldest Christian nation in the world and the background of Chris-tianity, and how it came to this country, is of utmost im-portance to the entire realm of history in Armenia."

Past the computer room, which contains the eleven computers and a huge monitor for the teacher, is a large room. "In the winter months, this is where we do physical training. We all use this room – students, teachers and staff. We all need to stay in good health. The school even has a folk dancing group, which consists mainly of teachers. There are, however, some students. When they saw the teachers having such a good time, they also wanted to learn. It is all about the *spirit* of learning here. I even dance with them and we go to many events to dance. It is traditionally a part of our culture.

"Music and art are an extremely strong part of the education, with much emphasis being put on creativity. Students learn to be proud of their individualism and to create with their own minds."

The library, though more like a large closet than a room, is fully stocked with books. "Like the physical training here, **everyone** uses the library . . . not only the students, teachers and staff, but also the workers," he is quick to note. "The woman who cleans the school even uses it and she has ten children."

"Ten?" asks one of the visitors in shock. "How does someone with ten children have time to read?"

As most of the group comment on that is probably the only quiet time the mother has, another asks, "How does she have ten children?"

"Heroism, I call it!" answers Hakobyan. "She is an amazing person and does good work." That part of his comment is visible from the appearance of the entire school building.

Outside is the regular area for physical training. There are two basketball goals, needing nets, and two handball goals, with nets. "The students made these themselves. There is no money for these items so they took what they could find and made them." From the look on the visitors' faces, it is a safe bet that basketball nets will be included in the next shipment from North Carolina to Armenia.

Hakobyan, like everyone else in the country, invites everyone into his office for coffee. "Take your place," he says as the traditional coffee and chocolates are brought in. He takes pleasure in pointing out that the ring-binder notebooks he received from Project AGAPE a couple of days prior are already in his office and in use by himself, the teachers and the staff. The next few moments are spent chatting and basking in the details of the morning.

This visit to School #2 in disputed territory brings about a life-changing lesson for all who have witnessed the facility and met Hakobyan and seen the teachers and staff. It brings awareness to the fact that less is definitely more. Although the classrooms are more primitive than America's rooms of the 1950s, there is a 99.6% literacy rate here. The students have only a copybook (possibly depending on the grade level), a few pencils and a couple of pens. There is no long list of supplies, so there is less to lose. There is no security necessary. "Like your friend as you would yourself" is on the wall, acting as their security. The teachers— all female—are professionally dressed and in heels, even on their workday, except for the physical education teacher who is still smartly dressed. The students make their own handball goals and basketball goals, and everything with which they do any type of physical activity here at the school. It is the same with the dance classes. The students make their own native costumes from the sewing supplies they receive. Thanks to the clothing, toiletries and the few necessary school supplies provided by Project AGAPE, these students are all receiving a first-class education and preparation for university work in the years ahead.

As a coda to all that has been seen and heard during the morning, Hakobyan adds, "All children here go to school. Students attend school six days a week. That is a requirement, we have no control over it and it is supported by the parents. I do not understand how students can do with less days than that. They also study their education with a book at home.

"We have had lunch already for the past five or six years for the students. Every student gets a cake and a cup of milk at the lunch break. That is a gift for them. They do not pay for it."

The words of that statement are immediately heart-wrenching yet at the same time, send a delayed message that during the first years following the Azeri War, students spent all day at school with no lunch. Hakobyan, unaware that his words have sent a chill of pained reality through the listeners, continues. "An American made that bridge ("bridged the gap," in our terminology) between America and Berdzor. He gets that meal for students. It's fantastic!" It is soon understood, with a bit more clarification, that the cake is actually a small cake of bread that is served with a cup of milk each school day. The realization is humbling.

One of the team asks another question. "Does the school also participate in competitive sports with other schools?"

"Ah, yes!" Hakobyan answers without hesitation. There is a great deal of animation in his voice. "My wife is the teacher of physical training." He beams in the same way as a proud American father speaking of his star athlete. "She is the trainer of handball and, I must say, she is exceptional. She trains the team from all of Karabagh that competes both in Yerevan and abroad. She very often brings home medals. She always wins." His pride is for both the school and his wife's prestigious career in the sport.

"There are different teams made up of different grades," he goes on to explain, "but the older grades are on the team that competes."

Hakobyan shows off the "medals" which are simply a paper certificate, possibly with a bit of ribbon. Some even have a large ribbon, something like place awards in America. There are no huge trophies, but that matters not. The students are just as proud of their paper and ribbon "medals" as if they had come home with a towering trophy. Suddenly, even more so than with the classrooms, the difference between education and appreciation here and in the United States becomes real. That awareness causes yet another question.

"What made you decide to come here?" Though asked by one person, the faces of each person in the room seem hungering to know exactly what prompted such an intelligent man to leave a successful lifestyle and come here, to an area totally different from his background. It is a certainty that each of them understands "the bleeding heart" syndrome, or else they would not be here, in this place serving as a representative and active proponent of missions and mission work. Probably each of them knows at least one person from the States who has gone to a mission area to serve a year or two, but Hakobyan's case is different. Why he—like the vet and all of the other workers connected to the schools, clinics and Project AGAPE—has come and stayed at least ten years or longer is a dedication of servanthood to be admired.

"After the earthquake and the war, when our soldiers freed these areas but many died in the effort, who would be here to carry on what they had worked so hard to do? Only the people like us. If I had not come to work with the children, and to do my part in supporting Nagorno-Karabakh, then all the men that died here . . . it would have been in vain." His face is filled with remorse. "Many men gave up their lives here. The least I could do was to come here and help educate their children and try to help those who were left. It is my way of offering a better life . . . hope.

"I have a house in Yerevan and I could work there, but I decided of course to come here, to my 'home.' Home to a part of the land that was once our homeland. Home to the place where my ancestors once lived and owned the land. I thought so much and often about *who* would carry on the work of those soldiers. 'Who,' I finally asked myself, 'if I don't? Who else?'"

He pauses for a moment, leaving one to question whether he is giving a moment of silence for those brave souls who lost their lives here, or to allow the impact of his words to penetrate the air. "They didn't take me to war because of my age, but I could come after the Azeri War and I did. Most of us who are here at Project AGAPE and working within the schools and with the families in any capacity thought so. They all felt the same way. The teachers all come from different places in Armenia, to be here and work in Nagorno-Karabakh too.

"What we think about is what would happen if none of us came here to work? Then the loss of our soldiers' lives would have been in vain. And had my family lived here, in the Lachin Corridor (Berdzor), prior to the war, I'd certainly want to live here now.

"And it wasn't just the Azeri war," he admits. A hint of grief sweeps over his face, casting an eerie somberness in the air like an invisible shadow. "Every family in Armenia had members affected by the genocide. No matter what part of the country they lived in, all were affected. I'll tell you this . . ." His words die off and are followed by several moments of silence. Words are unnecessary; everyone present is suddenly enveloped by a sense of the struggles of occupation, exploitation and death, war and hostility—all a part of Armenia's long history of survival—as real as if the images were shown on the wall. Yet as the expression on Hakobyan's experienced face transforms from one of sorrowful gloom to one of sincere gratitude and appreciation, his expression—again without words—conveys exactly what makes Project AGAPE so special and why it is so extremely important to this disputed territory. His expression and smile are filled with the same confident optimism, the same anticipation and expectation that help to raise the people of Karabakh above their despair. "By being here, I can offer these students a world of hope . . . of peace. And, most especially," he adds with an earnest smile, "God's love for all humankind." His words and tone speak of the very principles on which Project AGAPE was founded and operates, of offering healing to a world of brokenness. As an educator, this role is his way of bringing hope and peace to the people of this disputed territory, for what the students learn at school, they carry home to their families.

"The best thing in all of our country is education,"

Hakobyan continues. "Our minds are our greatest assets. For what should the Armenians do if we do not think? We have no big factories, no industries. Only our minds can help us, I think. We have no big mines to get something from underground to sell, for we have no natural resources in the ground. We have to sell our minds, our brains.

"Many would say that most of the Armenians went to America, either during or after the genocide, as a part of the Diaspora. Their goal was to leave their sons and so on, anyone who arrived there, to find their American dream." He pauses for a moment as he stares directly into the eyes of the visitors. "But the American dream is not what it once was. Yes?" he questions, without waiting for a reply. "Yes," he concludes with a slight nod.

A contemplative expression then comes over Hakobyan's face, a hint that, once again, whatever is on his mind is troubling to him. He looks down at the table for a moment before looking back up to speak. "I was watching the television one night. It was a program where they were talking about Ireland and they were interviewing an Irish man who had left his home country to make his fortune, to find his American dream. I distinctly remember his comment . . ." He paused in an effort to recall the man's exact words, '. . . I came to America and I got everything, but I lost what I had.'"

Prophetic does not begin to describe what Hakobyan has just expressed. The comment reverberates through the air, over and over, haunting the soul until the truth of the statement is not only heard but thoroughly understood and grasped by the listeners as one of "life's most important lessons." For not only are the Irish man's words true regarding what had once been termed "the American dream," but also for so many other situations in life where people chase their dreams. They get to the mountaintop and have lost everything of true value on the way there. These are words that the people of Nagorno-Karabakh truly understand and live. They are also words that are a focal point for the way Project AGAPE facilitates the residents and agencies of Kashatagh - "Raise them up, but don't leave what is theirs behind."

"This, too, is why I have come here and why I work here. Education is all we have to offer our children and I want to make sure they have every opportunity for that. They are owed that in spite of the earthquake, the fall of the Soviet Union, and the Azeri war."

Again there is complete silence, for what response can one make to that? It is Hakobyan who finally speaks again. "I have forgotten to tell one thing about the school, if you don't mind. Project AGAPE, I must say, gives us the copy books once or twice a year, and also some pens and a few school supplies for the children. But one year I even asked Nara to give us cloth for making a flag for Nagorno-Karabakh with the students. She brought the cloth and gave it to the school, along with everything we needed. So the school made a flag of the length of 10 meters, and wide in 4 or 5 meters. It is a huge flag. And it is an enormous pride not only of our school, but for the whole area of Kashatagh. If there is any kind of special occasion, we bring it and wave it proudly.

"The flag is amazing!" he exclaims so excitedly that

one can almost feel the energized exuberance from the crowds at its appearance." We also made ties for the students. And we use those also for special occasions. Nara even gave us a sewing machine to make all of these things, for it was only with the aid of it that we were able to make all of them.

"When I told her how very much we appreciated the gift of the sewing machine, she was most humble and her response was, 'It was not such a big thing as you say.' She's a woman like that. Nara does many things and helps many people, yet she takes no credit for any of it.

"You can look at her and know she is where God put her. She desired to be an Ambassador, and that is exactly what she is as she works as the Country Director of Project AGAPE. They give help to the families and clothes to the students so they can go to school. When working with her while I was the Assistant Director of the Christian Education Center, I watched closely as she was distributing the items. What I saw was that she was happier offering the help than were those who received the help. That is why I say she is truly a special woman. Her heart is here. And she has a good staff, a very good staff."

What a powerful individual speaking also of another powerful individual, both of them walking humbly in their paths doing the work God has set before them. There is nothing one can say after that so the visitors make their way quietly back to the front entrance of the school, stopping only to offer thanks for the gift of Hakobyan's time and hospitality.

As the visitors exit the building, Hakobyan is quick

to point out that the plants in the landing are cared for by the students as a part of their studies. "Nothing goes unused and everything has a purpose." The same can be said for each bright-minded child who enters these doors.

The visit to the school opens one's eyes to many aspects of learning and instruction, particularly the fact that it is not about what you have, but how you relay the information and the attitude and professionalism with which it is presented. More importantly, it provides an inside and stirring account of the Armenian people and their values, This school may be in a disputed territory of the world, but as to the wealth of knowledge and level of education that the students are receiving—thanks greatly to Project AGAPE and its supporters, as well as the dedicated individuals the administration employs—there is no dispute.

PART FIVE

THE LIFE TO COME

MAKING IT HAPPEN

CHAPTER 29

The Greatest Gift

This book is filled with accounts of help given by Project AGAPE and the many blessings received during that process. It says little, however, of the numerous and immeasurable stories of how the project reciprocally changed the lives of the ones who have gone there to serve. They are the ones who receive the greatest gift, for indeed, "We Are Blessed to Be a Blessing," as are the words of the title of a song by David Piner, Executive Director of Arbor Acres Retirement Community in Winston-Salem, North Carolina, a United Methodist facility. Thus it seems only appropriate to share a few of the comments from the missioners . . . the persons who had a hand—literally—in "making it happen for the children of the ark."

Although the events and personal stories contained in this book are somewhat heartrending, they point to a country in great need and the response to that need. Many of the readers of this book will be of the generation who knows of the Iron Curtain or the Soviet Union, and will remember its fall. But how many will actually understand and appreciate the full impact, even after reading this book and learning of the aid administered by Project AGAPE? Perhaps the strongest comment to bring that point home is one quoted earlier by Rev. Charles Davis during an interview. "What people fail to understand is that when the Soviet Union fell, *everything* fell."

The event entailed in that one sentence causes one to stop and think of the ripple effect that will be set into motion by that one instance. Then to realize that it is sandwiched between an earthquake that literally caused complete villages to fall, killing at least 25,000—more if you count the ones who later die due to related circumstances— and a war with Azerbaijan that left hundreds and hundreds of fallen soldiers lying all over the ground of their native motherland. It is unfathomable for anyone in most of the world to grasp the horror and despair left for the people who inhabited that country.

Years later, a woman who travels to Nagorno-Karabakh to serve persons of the area, particularly the residents of Project AGAPE's Children's Home, through her profession of dentistry shares this recollection: "Armenia wasn't easy to get into, easy to live in or easy to get out of, but my ten-day stay there was one of the best times of my getting-longer-everyday life. As many of those close to me know, for the past few years I had sustained a dream of going to the country that first recognized Christianity as the state religion. I must give my mother-in-law, Betty Cordes, credit for planting the seeds of curiosity and love for this beleaguered country. Her grandmother immigrated to the US sometime during the Armenian genocide.

"I was truly sorry to leave, a fact I would not have believed when I first arrived. The spirit of the people with whom I came in contact, those with whom I worked, those I observed working to restore this struggling place to order, was an inspiration. They take no pity on themselves, focus on what is good and right with their lives, and celebrate all that God has given them. Park Astdzo! Praise the Lord!" - - - Elizabeth H. Cordes, DDS

It is indeed heartwarming to know that there is a great partnership between The United Methodist Church and the Armenian Apostolic Church in America, as well as in Armenia. There are two amazing individuals, Harry Moorachian and Mary (Maro) Telfeyan, both of whom are a part of the Armenian Diaspora living in America and are not too far away from the Saint Sarkis Armenian Apostolic Church in Charlotte, North Carolina, where they initially learn of Project AGAPE. (Saint Sarkis is the first, and only, Armenian Apostolic Church between Richmond, Virginia, and Charleston, South Carolina). With their ancestral roots, this is instantly of interest to them. Both Harry (who has served on the Board of Directors and has visited Project AGAPE), and Mary (who currently serves on the Board of Directors but has never been to her native homeland) are tremendous supporters of Project AGAPE in a different way, always willing to educate and tell more people about it and the work being done in Nagorno-Karabakh.

Because of the ages of Mary's children, it is not currently feasible for her to visit the project, but she sings the praises of the work being done there, and of Cecil Donahue and Allan van Meter. Cecil is the former Chairperson of the Board of Directors and Allan is the current one. "Cecil and Allan are wonderful people. I cannot say enough about them and the way the board is run. The infrastructure of the board, in conjunction with the work they do through Project AGAPE is amazing. They are extremely knowledgeable of the Armenian culture and traditions, and make sure that any work done does not detract from that. Another thing that is impressive is how The United Methodist Church partners with the Armenian Apostolic Church. The entire concept is remarkable and carried out well."

Rene Henderson, a three-time mission worker with Project AGAPE, tells a story that describes exactly how the Armenian people are. Everyone interviewed in the course of this book shares the exact same sentiment, "They are the most hospitable people I have ever met anywhere in the world."

Her following account attests to that. "My husband and I had a brief respite from our work one day and decided to visit the war memorial in Berdzor. We were climbing the steps to the top and saw an older lady there sweeping the steps. We did not speak Armenian and she did not speak English but we managed to smile and convey a greeting to one another. We continued to the top, lingered briefly to offer prayers of gratitude for those who gave their lives in the war and for the gift of the opportunity to serve the people in Berdzor. We descended the steps and again met our new friend about half way down. It was just past noon and she was unfolding a cloth with her lunch inside. She motioned for us to join her and offered to share her lunch, which consisted of a small amount of bread and cheese. She was so earnest and sincere in her insistence that we felt it would have been rude to refuse. Her graciousness was so apparent, language barrier notwithstanding. We were touched deeply by her hospitality, true Christian hospitality, giving what little she had to strangers. We shared her bread and cheese, hugged and thanked her, and returned to the AGAPE compound. I've served in the US and in other countries on mission trips, but I've not had this experience before or since."

Rene's interest in Armenia is first piqued when her cousin marries an Armenian girl from Fresno, California, and they become fast friends. In Rene's words, "It is not until many years later that she told me about the Armenian genocide, her grandmother's story of escape, and her father's return to his village to help build schools. I had never heard of the Armenian genocide. She told me how she went to Armenian school growing up and every year the older kids would go on a work team to Armenia. I was taken in by her family when I visited and introduced to Armenian foods, religion, culture and music. The more I learned, the more I wanted to know and to visit.

"I began an online search to find a mission team near Charlotte, North Carolina, where I lived by this time. My search turned up Project AGAPE through the Western

North Carolina Conference of The United Methodist Church. *I am a long time Methodist and this is my conference!* I immediately began the application process, recruited my best friends—a contractor and an architect—and we went on our first trip to help build houses. We worked putting the roof on a house, installing the ceiling and general site clean-up around the house where we were working. The three of us returned the next year in the same capacity. I went alone the third time and worked with a team on the staff house on the Project AGAPE compound."

When asked about the memorable part of her trips, Rene is quick to respond, "Meeting the people of Berdzor and surrounding communities. As I told Bishop Goodpaster (Bishop of the Western North Carolina Conference of The United Methodist Church), I have never met such people. They were so gracious, giving the best they had to offer in hospitality, not out of plenty but out of scarcity—a rare virtue in my experience. No one ever asked me for anything, but instead tried to give me something. The homeowners were eager to help us build or repair their houses, as were their friends and neighbors. We were a large team the first two of my three visits, and yet were outnumbered by Armenian volunteers."

Like everyone else who visits or works at Project AGAPE, playing with the children—especially those of the Children's Home—is always a highlight. "By the third year I had learned some Armenian. The children were patient teachers and gracious in refining my pronunciation."

A mission trip to Project AGAPE also incorporates tours of historic sites along the highway on the way to

Berdzor from Yerevan. "I loved every minute and every-thing we saw," admits Rene. "We ate at Armenian restau-rants and visited market squares and centuries old churches. We were greeted in a friendly but unobtrusive manner everywhere we went. I love Armenia—the food, the history, the geography, their philosophy of life, and yes even their difficult language that I would love to master some-day—but most of all, I love the people."

Regarding Project AGAPE's greatest asset and great-est need, as seen from the eyes and experiences of a missioner, Rene offers an incredibly comprehensive an-swer. "Their greatest asset is Nara Melkonyan. I see fund-ing of Project AGAPE as the greatest need. Nara uses every resource and squeezes every bit of worth from every penny sent. I am in awe of her resourcefulness, business savvy, and diplomacy. On speaking tours in the US, Nara presents the needs of the people in a dignified manner, not begging for money and goods, but rather educating people about the conditions of the Karabakh region and why the condi-tions persist. This builds a relationship through empathy rather than sympathy.

"I cannot foresee a 'fix' for the geopolitical problems of Karabakh in the near future. In the meantime, what are the people of the region to do . . . continue a subsistence existence? If we do not help with our money, our goods, our prayers, and by spreading the word to educate people that this place and these wonderful people exist, what then? Not everyone can go or wants to go but we can make it personal by telling our stories of the children of the Children's Home—Haikuhy, Agnessa, Ani, Haik. We can tell the stories of the homeowners working alongside us, protecting us from the more dangerous jobs—Gago, Hamest, Maria. We can tell the stories of the doctors and nurses of the hospital who do their best to take care of patients with few resources and old equipment. I may not be able to go again, which breaks my heart, but perhaps now that I have gone, my money would be better spent in the form of regular contributions in an amount I can afford that will go directly and 100 percent to the project."

Linda Erlandson is a six-time veteran of working at Project AGAPE. As both a team participant *and* a team leader over her years of service, she wears many hats. But whether putting on roofs, installing windows, renovating kitchens, installing toilets, unloading a shipment containing hundreds of Christmas Shoeboxes among its load, or enjoying a free afternoon with the children of the Children's Home, she understands she is where she is called to be. Now as a member of the Board of Directors for Project AGAPE, she can still be involved with the work there even when she is home in America.

Her first trip, in 2004, involves working on a combination orphanage/day care center in Stepanakert, the capital of Nagorno-Karabakh. The orphanage, established for children orphaned by the war in the 1990s, is started by five Armenian women who see a need and act on it. At first they receive no financial help, but they later receive a very small salary from the government, $25.00 to $50.00 per month for the teachers and director.

Located in an extremely rundown building once used as an Old Soldiers' Home, the orphanage has malfunctioning bathroom facilities. The small room containing the two bath tubs has only an exterior door. The building team from North Carolina guts the bathroom and installs tiles and new fixtures. An interior door is created for the tub room and the exterior door is walled up. To stabilize the water supply, which came intermittently from a pipe in the yard, the team erects a water reservoir tank next to the building.

While there in 2004, the team sees a great need to renovate the kitchen. The cook feeds the 30 children, the staff, and the team using a stove with only one working burner. The rest of the kitchen is in equally poor shape. Linda takes a team back to the orphanage in 2005 to gut and rebuild the kitchen.

"What calls you back again and again?" Linda is asked.

"It is simply the people. My enduring fondness for Nara, her family, and the Project AGAPE staff; witnessing their sacrifices and hardship to help the people of Berdzor and especially the children are what compel me to return again and again. It is the least I can do to share my love, service, and money to support the Project AGAPE efforts."

The memorable experiences of adult missioners are interesting and enlightening, but what do they mean to a teenager, a young lady preparing for her senior year of high school? What is it like to leave the role of being Senior Class President in a prominent school? Of being amidst other teens who have their own vehicles, the latest technological gadgets, designer clothes and accessories, pedicures and manicures, arts and entertainment, shopping malls - not to mention restaurants and fast food galore on every corner . . . then suddenly land in the middle of the night at an airport shrouded by darkness as you travel to a country of not only dire poverty but in a disputed territory?

For Courtney Beals, who is 17 at the time of her 2013 summer mission trip to Armenia and Nagorno-Karabakh, it is an eye-opening experience. Not a rude awakening, but an enriching transformation, as you can sense from her words. "This past summer, I was blessed with the opportunity to be a part of a mission team traveling overseas to Armenia in the Kashatagh region of Nagorno-Karabaugh. After hearing, in the fall of 2012, of my church's decision to send a mission team overseas, I immediately knew this was something I wanted to be a part of. Mission work is something I see myself being actively engaged in in the future so I decided to use a portion of my trip as my senior project. I expressed interest and started laying the ground work to make this trip a reality.

"Though I was touched by so many people over the course of two weeks in Armenia, the children at the orphanage made the biggest impact on my life. The orphanage was located directly up the road from our compound, making it a place that I could frequent easily. Working through a language barrier, I was able to organize activities similar to a Bible School for the 22 children taking refuge at the AGAPE Children's Home; incorporating singing, coloring activities, and different Bible stories. Though the children were able to learn from me, I gained so much from them. More than anything, I think they exposed me to what true love is. The children were from broken homes and many had experienced trials that I couldn't image surviving. The children's living conditions were much less than what we, as Americans, are accustomed to. In most homes, running water was a novelty. Housing was very inadequate, especially for the cold weather this region experiences. Though their living conditions and situations were much less than fortunate, all the children and people I came into contact with were extremely gracious beyond belief. They were a people full of God's love and they let this show in every aspect of their lives."

Different people, same comments. That is what one gets when speaking to anyone who has served on a mission trip to Nagorno-Karabakh. Different time, same comments. Whether visits to Armenia happen in 1992 or 2013, responses are all the same. One time or several times, same comments. No matter whether a missioner pays a single visit to Armenia or returns for a total of seven trips, the responses are always the same.

Well, **almost** always the same. There is **one** interesting addition to the collection of "missioner" stories that possesses a different, and compassionately memorable, reaction. Some missioners do physical work either on building teams, medical or dental teams, VBS teams, and any other type of team that requires going to a mission site to work on a project. There are also those who, physically unable to go, make a monumental difference through a monetary gift. Such is the case of one very special missioner-from-home whose impact on the work of Project AGAPE cannot be ignored, nor forgotten. The following report is told by Nara Melkonyan, and collaborated by Mark

Kushigian, the son of the man who makes a long-lasting and meaningful contribution to a major accomplishment in AGAPE's assistance to an entire village.

"During my first trip to North Carolina in May of 1999," relates Nara, "I was taken to St. Paul's United Methodist Church in Asheville. After my presentation, two of the attendees—a father and son—approached me and wanted to talk with me. After we greeted each other I asked the father, 'Are you Armenian?'

"He answered, 'Yes, how did you know that?'"

"I replied, 'Your Armenian nose prompted me.'"

"He smiled and said, 'It's not good to say that.'"

"'My nose is similar to yours and I am not ashamed of it,' I responded jokingly. We both laughed and he (his last name was Kushigian) started asking some details about the water project in Bagaran.

"Later Alec Alvord told me that Mr. Kushigian donated $15,000.00 to the Bagaran water project. He died shortly after that with cancer. I don't know how long he was sick, but my inner voice says to me that he knew he was going to die and wanted to 'pay' his last 'tribute' to his motherland."

Mark Kushigian, the son who was with his father at St. Paul's UMC for Nara's presentation, shares this addendum and tidbit of interesting background to the beautifully touching story of his father's mission work experience. "My father was born in Detroit, Michigan, in 1922 to Armenian parents who fled the genocide in Turkey. He died in November 1999 and only officially knew he had cancer for one month before he died. Did he know he was going to die? Medically speaking, no. But maybe somehow, yes."

A connecting element throughout the entirety of this book is the continual response of "God's hand" to miraculous happenings. In this case, the appropriate response is "God's hand, Mr. Kushigian's heart."

The people, the children of the ark, are born of the same stock. Legend has it that ancient Armenians had red hair and blue eyes. That is certainly not the case of today. For the most part, they have dark hair and incredibly striking dark—almost to the point of being black—almond-shaped eyes. But no matter their appearance, their hearts and their hospitality are what shine through. Their generosity of what little they have is what one remembers. Their desire to help themselves is the trait that sticks in one's mind. ***The people.***

For Sandy Waldron, one of the first Americans to set foot in Armenia following its approximately 70-year history of being under Communist rule, another trip to Armenia is always in the back of her mind. Laughing, she continues to joke, "I still say I got to Armenia because I could drive a bus." But from the very first day she encounters the four Armenian men in Suzanne Stafford's class at the School of Christian Living, she recognizes that the work in Armenia and Nagorno-Karabakh—which grows into Project AGAPE—is a God-blessed project. She still holds that same viewpoint today.

Nara, who laughingly responds to Sandy's comment about the bus, says, "And I got to Project AGAPE because of a copy machine!" There is no doubt in her mind that God placed her where He wanted her to be. The project, its work and the people are her life.

Rev. Charles Davis fondly remembers those early days, a time when "for everything I did, Sam Dixon did something too. He is the one who made it happen. Suzanne Stafford and Sam are the reason Project AGAPE got off the ground." Charles looks down. "I always regret not having gone on that trip to Haiti in 2010 with him. He asked, but I told him I was getting too old for that. I was actually in a medical care facility a few months later when I heard he'd been killed when the earthquake hit Haiti."

Ann, Charles' wife, interjects, "Charles was in a Life Care Center in Rocky Mount, North Carolina, getting IVs everyday due to an infection he'd gotten in his hip. They'd actually had to remove his hip at the hospital to let it heal, and he had to stay in a round-the-clock care facility until the hip healed and was able to be replaced. When the news of Sam's death arrived, we were fearful of what it would do to Charles. My daughter, son-in-law and Charles' nurse went in with me to tell him, for we knew it was going to be on television and would terribly upset him."

An expression of thoughtful reminiscence is on Charles' face as he reiterates, "The success of Project AGAPE is largely due to Sam's help."

Everyone connected with the birth of Project AGAPE speaks of those early days with fondness and love. Yet their compassion and mission does not start there. Charles Wesley, one of the world's greatest hymn writers and brother of John Wesley, penned a text in 1742 that could just as easily speak of the mission of Project AGAPE. The words carry a truth that has been, is, and ever shall be –

from the creation of Mount Ararat to Noah's call from God
and to our call now.

Help Us to Help Each Other

Help us to help each other, Lord,
each other's cross to bear,
let each his friendly aid afford,
and feel each other's care.

What better words to pray to God as we strive—
whether in our own congregations, locally, statewide, nationally or in worldwide settings like Armenia—to raise
others up?

CHAPTER 30

A Letter of Gratitude to Project AGAPE

The final chapter of a book always creates the strenuous task of pulling together all the other chapters and tying them off, bringing closure or an ending to the act of telling the story. It is somewhat like a balloon filled with air, fun to enjoy or let soar, but all the air inside must be captured and tied together with a knot or it can do neither; it is useless. Such are the closing words of any book, be it novel or non-fiction.

Bearing that in mind, there is no better way to tie that final knot in this book than to actually share the words

264

of a young Armenian woman, now in college in Yerevan, who has grown up in the Berdzor area, knowing the assistance and love of Project AGAPE while instilling her life with a sense of hope and joy. This letter, in the words of Elinar Hairapetyan, epitomizes the work of AGAPE and the love it gives to all of Karabakh through the hands of those who support it.

A LETTER OF GRATITUDE TO PROJECT AGAPE FOR ALL HAPPY MOMENTS

I had just started to go to school. One day my father came home with two big boxes. I remembered well especially one of those, because when I opened that box with my brothers, a boundless joy "wrapped" me. There were many soft toys in the box. I cherish those toys till the present, they are the memories of the happy moments of my childhood, the decorations of my room.

At that time I didn't know where the gifts were from. Several years later I started to attend the computer classes at the AGAPE Center. One time there were visiting Americans at AGAPE. We were getting ready to have a special event for them. I had never opened an English textbook in the school, but my interest was so big, I wanted so much to communicate with them, but I couldn't as I didn't understand them.

After some efforts I found a conversational dictionary and started to learn it reading even during the time I was walking to AGAPE Center to participate in the special event for the guests. Even greeting them in English was a big joy for me. I remember I met one of the guests at the AGAPE gate. I told him, "How do you do?"

He replied to me and told, "You happy?" I didn't understand him, but smiled as a reply. He took two photos out of his pocket, showed me and said, "This is my son and this is my daughter, they also dance."

It was time to start the performance for the guests, who had already gathered to watch it. I was dancing in a dancing group. Our dancing teacher Anna had taught us a modern and an Armenian dance to perform. I was looking forward to the end of the performance, because there was an African American among the guests and I wanted to invite her to dance. My childhood dream was to dance in a dancing group where African Americans dance, because I always admired their dance technique. I can tell that my dream partially came true that day, because at the end of the performance children invited the guests to dance. I invited the African American to dance, too. I was dancing with her and feeling so happy, so joyful, though we couldn't understand each other. At the end we received gifts from the guests and we said good-bye to them.

I opened the bag with gifts at home and the most interesting for me was the letter and a photo with it. There was a group of children in a classroom in the photo. That photo found a special place in my photo album. I hope one day I will see those children to express my gratitude, and not only that: I may also suggest them to make a movie about AGAPE and call it "One of those good days at AGAPE" or just "AGAPE," as that name sounds good.

Even after graduating the computer classes we had always been invited to special events at AGAPE Center. And we had always had a very interesting time there. During the events children would always get gifts. And then our parents would go to get aid from the Project. And I would get more soft toys and nice memories.

I was about to forget the most important thing: I gathered all the notebooks received from AGAPE in order to use those when going to college. And now the scenarios of my future movies took place in those notebooks, as I entered the Yerevan State College of Culture, the department of movie production. I was living in Yerevan, but getting clothes from AGAPE in Berdzor. I had always been looking forward to getting the nice clothes from my Mother, received from AGAPE. I was wearing those and going to college with pleasure, as the other students seeing me in those, told me, "The American is coming."

My clothes were different from other's and I was happy that only I had those and no one had clothes like mine. I say a heartfelt "THANK YOU" to YOU ALL and, thanks to AGAPE, I remember the days of my childhood with joy. And thanks to you, I got straight "A's" for my English classes in the school. I wish you all happiness and big love.

I cannot find better words to express my gratitude, because regardless how much I write, you deserve much more than that.

With boundless love,

Elinar Hairapetyan

EPILOGUE

The historic, and very familiar, Biblical account of the land of Ararat begins with God calling on Noah. It is not just any ordinary call, but a very specialized one . . . a call now known (and known for centuries before) to man, woman and child . . . anyone who is remotely familiar with the Bible and the stories that come from ancient times.

That call, from Genesis 7:1 (NRSV), reads, "Then the Lord said to Noah, 'Go into the ark, you and all your household, for I have seen that you alone are righteous before me in this generation." The rest of that story concludes in Genesis 7:5 with the words, "And Noah did all that the Lord had commanded him."

Noah's answer to that call has impacted the lives of all generations since that time. Noah's answer to that call is still making it happen for all of us – the "Children of the Ark" today. How will we, then, answer our call to make it happen for the people of Nagorno-Karabakh, not only for today, but for all the tomorrows to come? May we continue to play a role in raising up the children and the inhabitants of the Kashatagh province through Project AGAPE as we realize our own blessings and turn to God with thanks, saying, "You raise me up!"

A Closing Note from the Author

In the cargo compartment of the airplane, as I leave Armenia, is a large framed print of a 4th century church of Nagorno-Karabakh. It is a gift from Suren Khachatryan, governor of the Kashatagh region of this disputed territory. That church still stands even though it has withstood several bombings during its long rich history, and now boasts four levels of construction that have taken place over the many centuries. In a box with it is some lovely turquoise jewelry handmade by Nara's sister, Lusine; an obsidian cross necklace from Hakob Gumbalyan's son, Narek; an artistic sketch of me done by Agnessa (Boris' sister), one of the children at the AGAPE Children's Home, and a flag of Nagorno-Karabakh signed by the School #2 staff. These are a few of the treasured items I have accumulated along the way during the past five weeks. They are the items going home with me. In Nagorno-Karabakh, in exchange, is a piece of my heart.

The plane takes flight, headed to Rome, and as it leaves the ground, I get one last glimpse of the beloved Mount Ararat. As if orchestrated and right on cue, the clouds open and I am blessed with a breathtaking view of the landscaped treasure, as if it too has come to say, "Good-bye, dear friend." My eyes fill with tears as my heart and mind depart this now-familiar scene with the message, "You Raise Me Up, thou O Children of the Ark." I watch the mountaintop—of which I've heard about since my earliest memories in Sunday School—until it is no longer visible. Yet I know my experience of ascending the mountains of this disputed territory will never be out of my sight.

So yes, a piece of my heart is missing; I left it with the inhabitants of mountainous Kashatagh. But as for my body and soul, they have been raised to heights unknown by these children of the ark. These beautiful people have taught me so many invaluable lessons.

I envision the church print and the signed flag on my office wall, where they will be proudly displayed once I return home, and I know that for the rest of my days, they—like the Armenian Highlands, their inhabitants and especially the precious children—will continually raise me up.

Project AGAPE, its staff and all those whom it benefits have truly taught me a whole new meaning of the word love . . . it is appropriately called "AGAPE."

ABOUT THE PHOTOGRAPHER

Photographer Mark Barden is no stranger to capturing images on the foreign mission field. Since 2000, when he became the Director of Mission/Outreach for the Western North Carolina Conference of The United Methodist Church, he has used his telecommunications background to tell the stories of people all over the world. After becoming the WNCC Director of Communications in 2006, Mark continued to feed his passion for missions by volunteering on various mission trips, always bringing home a plethora of stories and photographs. From the jungles of the Democratic Republic of Congo and Sudan to the rice paddies of Cambodia to the snow-capped mountains of Armenia, he has continued to interweave the two of his greatest loves, missions and photography, into a tapestry that tells the story of God's love for all humanity.

Born into a Methodist parsonage family and a grandson of Methodist missionaries, Mark grew up with the church touching multiple aspects of his family's life. With a committed faith, along with degrees in communications, he followed God's calling into broadcast journalism and eventually college teaching at the University of Mississippi and Murray State University. Eventually his desire for parish ministry led him back to North Carolina to complete ministerial studies at Duke University. Currently, Mark is back in the parish as pastor of First United Methodist Church, Elkin, NC.

Mark is married to Barbara Jean Barden, Minister of Education at Myers Park United Methodist Church in Charlotte, NC. They have one son, Chris, a student at the University of North Carolina Charlotte.

ABOUT THE AUTHOR

Catherine Ritch is the author of 25 books, all of the inspirational genre, including fiction, non-fiction and children's titles. In addition, she is a composer and frequent speaker/musician for a wide range of conferences and events. After serving as an Organist/Minister of Music in local churches of the Western North Carolina Conference of The United Methodist Church for over 35 years, she now serves globally through her writing, speaking and music.

Whether on stage, dressed as comedienne Miz Eudora Rumph and portraying the simple mountain wit and wisdom of her Appalachian grandmother, or reaching out to those in need around the world—particularly in natural disaster areas—through her Rudy the Red Pig children's series, she loves bringing hope and laughter to others.

A radio personality once said of Ritch, "Catherine's lightning quick wit and musical talent are astonishing enough, but combined with her never ending source of positive energy, the woman is a ball of fire that is sure to inspire." Put Catherine on a piano, organ or keyboard and from Bach to Broadway to Boogie to the Best of Gospel, she'll have the audience enthralled with the rhythms of life.

Catherine lives in Stallings, North Carolina, only three miles from her childhood home. Her most treasured activity is spending time with her family, especially playing with the four younger grandchildren, aged four and under, who love books and music.